Chinese Vernacular Dwelling Cultural China Series

Cultural China Series

Chinese
Vernacular
Dwelling

Shan Deqi

Translated by Wang Dehua

CHINA
INTERCONTINENTAL
PRESS

图书在版编目（CIP）数据

  中国民居／单德启等著，王德华译.—北京：五洲传播出版社，2004.3
  ISBN 7-5085-0370-8

  I.中... II.①单... ②王... III.民居—建筑艺术—中国—英文 IV.TU241.5

中国版本图书馆 CIP 数据核字（2003）第 101635 号

中国民居

著　　者	单德启等
译　　者	王德华
责任编辑	孙海雯
责任校对	张行军
整体设计	海　洋
出版发行	五洲传播出版社（北京北三环中路31号　邮编：100088）
版式制作	张　红
承 印 者	北京华联印刷有限公司
开　　本	720×965毫米　1/16
字　　数	60千字
印　　张	9.5
版　　次	2004年3月第1版
印　　次	2004年3月第1次印刷
书　　号	ISBN 7-5085-0370-8/TU · 05
定　　价	85.00元

Contents

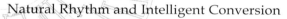
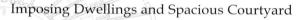
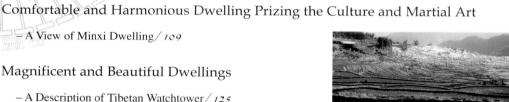

Introduction: Chinese Vernacular Dwelling

A land of peach blossoms: Xidi.

In the year 2000, Xidi and Hongcun, the ancient villages in Anhui Province of China were formally approved on the 24th session of UNESCO's World Heritage Committee to be inscribed into UNESCO's World Heritage List. In early spring of that year, the Japanese Expert Dr. Naomi Okawa, assigned by UNESCO's World Heritage Committee, highly valued the villages after his field investigation by saying that "it's really an unrivalled village scene such as Hongcun". "The village Xidi still remains its beautiful ancient streets and alleys, which is seldom in the world". In 1997, old town of Li Jiang in Yunnan Province and ancient city of Pingyao in Shanxi Province were inscribed into the World Heritage List; nowadays, the famous river town Zhouzhuang in Jiangsu Province is on application for the list. At the turn of the century, the Chinese traditional vernacular dwelling is unveiling itself to the world, becoming a big stage for China's access to the world and for the world to have a better understanding of China.

China is a country with vast territory, varied topography and diversified climate, together with its different kinds of nationalities and cultures, which creates a rich variety of settlements and buildings of

2

The screenwall of a quadrangle.

traditional vernacular dwelling. The residential houses can generally be divided into three patterns: courtyard, storied and caved (*or clay dwelling built with clay materials*) dwellings.

I

Courtyard dwelling is the most popular vernacular dwelling among all the patterns and it is also the one with most advanced material and structure technology, the richest component, most complicated arrangements of traditional ethic code and diversified decorations. In a sense, it is the most advanced dwelling style in the farming society and also the ideal mode to materialize the natural environment in the feudal society. The quadrangles in Beijing are the typical one of this pattern. The fundamental character of the courtyard dwelling is: being enclosed, symmetrical in middle axis and clear distinction between primary and secondary, outside and inside. Such kind of dwelling is mainly seen in North China, Central Plains, Shandong

The *Tu Zhang* Dwelling in Ailao Mountain region, Yunnan Province.

A quadrangle in Beijing.

Peninsula, plains and coastal areas in South China. It also can be found in some basins and plains of the southwest of China and in the areas of Chengdu in Sichuan Province, Kunming and Dali in Yunnan Province and plain areas of Taiwan Island, etc. The courtyard dwelling is popularly adopted in many areas including the areas where the Hans settle in, ethnic minority areas in close exchange with Han culture (such as the Bai and Nahsi nationalities) and some developed areas (such as Zhuang and Yi nationalities), or the ethnic minorities living with the Han nationality (such as

4

The color picture and carved decoration of a quadrangle.

The main gate of a quadrangle.

Manchu and Hui nationalities).

In marching into one of the international metropolises, laws have also been formulated in Beijing to protect its 25 lanes and quadrangles in the ancient areas, ranging from Prince Gong's Residential to common houses, which still have kept the most completed and almost whole forms of quadrangles of the courtyard dwelling. For example, as to the gate, there are *Naizi Fang* Gate, *Jinzhu* Gate, *Brilliant* Gate, *Ruyi* Gate, *Manzi* Gate and so on, which make up the real museum of the quadrangle. Businessmen in Shanxi Province were in the leading position in building private residential in the period of the Ming and Qing dynasties. The Quadrangle Group of the Wang family

The quadrangle group of the Wang family in Shanxi Province.

The patio in Huizhou dwelling.

in Lingshi County, known as the First House of Shanxi Province, is composed of over one hundred courtyards. Despite of variation in scale, composition, decoration and other aspects, all the quadrangles, which are most popular in the northern plain areas, have the common fundamental characteristics, such as the famous Confucian Residence in Qufu (Shandong Province), Zheng Banqiao's Former Residence in Weifang (Shandong Province) and the numerous old-style banking houses in the ancient city of Pingyao in Shanxi Province, etc. The dwellings in the vast countryside are not as complete as the typical quadrangle; some dwellings only have three or two houses around a courtyard, such as the Manchu's sun-facing rural dwelling in Liaoning and Jilin Provinces, *Tu Wei Zi* in Shaanxi and Shanxi Provinces, all of which are of

The Clay Building of Western Fujian Province.

simplified courtyard-dwelling categories remaining the basic structure of gate, wall, courtyard and central room and wing-room. There are many variation forms of such a courtyard dwelling as follows: the residential dwelling called *Yi Ke Yin* in Kunming, Yunnan Province, which generated from the cave uncalcined clay dwelling; Huizhou's courtyard residential dwelling (In Chinese traditional architecture, the courtyard enclosed by the houses and walls was called *tianjing* in Chinese) in Anhui Province, which came from the *ganlan* (In ancient times, this kind of architectural mode with wood as main building materials was popular in southern China) wood dwelling combined with courtyard ; and the Yongding's Hakka residential dwelling in Fujian Province, which was mainly built for self-defense under the specific historic and geographical circumstances; *Da Cuo* – a courtyard dwelling composed of red-brick wall, sloping roof and arc fireproof wall, made by immigrants from Guangdong and Fujian to Taibei area of Taiwan, and so on.

The earliest form of the courtyard dwelling emerged firstly in the period of Qin and Han dynasties, and the figure bricks in the Eastern Han Dynasty give us a complete form of the then courtyard dwelling. The widespread of such a dwelling culture was due to the technological supports of Qin's bricks and Han's tiles, the improvement of feudal farming family pattern and the popularization of etiquette norms. And in the long period of time of farming society, this vernacular dwelling pattern showed its extremely strong vitality.

II

Cave-style dwelling has explicitly regional characteristics in the natural ecology, remaining the most primitive architectural features among all vernacular dwelling patterns. The drought area in the Loess plateau in the northwest China is the area where the kind of dwellings most centralized.

The most typical cave-style dwelling is the Cave Dwelling which can be largely found in the middle and west regions including Henan, Shanxi, Shaanxi and Gansu, including the "underground Cave Dwelling" in the west of Henan and plains of

The Cave Dwelling.

southern Shaanxi – a kind of Cave Dwelling wholly built under the ground. Caves are dug with earth steps as entrance. This kind of dwelling is inhabited by several or a dozen of households and is still completely kept in Liquan County of Xi'an (Shaanxi Province); the "cliff-along" Cave Dwelling – another kind of Cave Dwelling widely adopted in mountainous regions and usually converged transversely and multiply along the contour line with connecting caves dug on natural hillsides and a courtyard can be built with adobe outside the cave; "plugging Cave Dwelling" – a mixed form

The Tibetan watchtower.

mostly appear in the middle of Shanxi with one or two storied arched adobe or brick house outside the cave and form a courtyard with walls, which seems more flexible in settlement combination and richer in inner space. And, there is a kind of semi-underground-cave dwelling remained in the settlements of Taiya and Yamei nationalities in Taiwan Province. Its shape is quite natural: generally with a rectangular flat covered with cobblestones and caved in about 1.5m, wood-framework upper structure using bamboo as purlin and being covered by day lily as roof. The whole settlement scattered loosely, which is believed to form in the long time of encountering typhoon, earthquake and other frequent disasters and remains till now. Despite of its

The Ganlan wood building.

limited space, there still has reserved the place for sacrifices in this kind of dwelling.

The Cave Dwelling, clay dwelling, or even the vernacular dwelling made of uncalcined clay, rammed earth, scattered in the drought or desert areas, such as *Zhuangguo* in the east of Qinghai Province, watchtower of Tibetan nationality in the areas of Sichuan, Qinghai and Tibet and even *Gaotai* vernacular dwelling in Kashi of the Xinjiang Uygur Autonomous Region, all belong to the category of uncalcined clay dwelling.

III

The Ganlan wood building is the typical storied dwelling, which distributes mostly in the mountains of minority nationalities in the southwest semi-tropical areas. Such a style has pushed the space form and space combination of storied dwelling, the support, suspension and stagger floor along the hills, and, the techniques of mortise and tenon to a very high level. It also demonstrates rich material and spiritual civilizations in combination with the unique national and folk cultures of the minority nationalities.

The traditional typical wood *Ganlan* buildings are all set up by wood including wood framework, wood purlin, plank wall, bark tile, with tenon and mortise at the link point, without any iron nail or iron hook. The plane of the house is rectangle, while the roof looks like double-slope shape, and the first two to three levels have no walls. The households live closely along the hillside. In the Dai nationality autonomous counties in Xishuangbanna in the southwest of Yunnan and De Hong in the west of Yunnan, there are bamboo *Ganlan* buildings with a kind of bamboo-wood-combined structure using large amount of *mao* bamboos. Compared with the wood one, the building material of bamboo dwelling are linked mostly by coir rope and rattan; its roof is called *Kongming's* Hat with swallow-tailed *Qianmu* – some kind like the *Xieshan*-style (*Roof of the Xieshan-style is composed of two big slopes at front and back and two small slopes at both sides, with two flats in the shape of isosceles triangle also being at both sides of the roof.*) four-slope roof. The Jingpo nationality, Jinuo nationality, Hani nationality and other minority nationalities in this area mostly adopt the bamboo dwelling. Their dwellings are alike in terms of the height of overhead level, whether they being paired up with the architecture materials (such as adobe, day lily, the tile top, etc.) and the worshiped totem

9

The drum tower at Ma'an Village, Sanjiang County, Guangxi.

The storm-tossed bridge of the Dong nationality.

except for slight differences. There are some other unique features of Yunnan's bamboo stockaded village, such as the Dais stockaded village, each of which has a well with painstaking decorations around or even with well pavilion or guardian stone-carving beast. Another example is the stockaded village gate of Hani nationality, which is always made of tree trunk and set in the entrance with fur on the cross wood and later bird carving instead. After numerous textual researches, Kenzaburo Torikoshi, the Japanese expert figured out that the traditional torii is derived from Yunnan. In addition, according to the building origin, fundamental framework and space idea, the *Diaojiao* building seen in the Mount Emei area in the southwest of Sichuan, Chongqing area and Fenghuang mountainous and lake areas in the west of Hunan Province are all the specific models of storied dwelling.

Dwelling in trees and dwelling in caves are both the most original modalities of Chinese traditional vernacular dwelling, which was once concluded by the ancient as "dwelling in trees in the south and caves in the north". The historical records and archaeological studies have fully proved that the *ganlan* wood building was once widely adopted in the areas south of Yangtze River, most of which are areas of mountains and hills with the humid, hot and rainy climate, the ecological resource of dense woods, the production mode of paddy cultivations. In ancient times, these regions were known as *Yue*s as a whole. The dwelling culture of *Ganlan* is the common feature of *Yue*s, and, the totem, courtyard, entrance and the subdivision of structure and materials together with the unique customs of all minorities, were passed on and formed such rich residential dwelling settlements in today's southern areas especially the southwest.

It is worth mentioning that with the growing population, declining wood resources, the popularization of architectural materials like brick and tile and some other factors, the Han nationality in the south and the minorities in the plains have increasingly farewell the *Ganlan* wood buildings, and progressed to many variations and new modalities, such as the water street dwelling in Zhejiang Province, the courtyard-style dwelling in Anhui Proivince, the adobe building in the south of Fujian Province, *Yi Ke Yin* in Kunming and so on.

The Chinese traditional vernacular dwelling always maximizes to comply with nature, or remake nature with compensation. As the polymer of vernacular dwelling, the emergence and development of traditional settlements have fully taken advantage

The vernacular dwellings of water street in Zhejiang Province.

of natural ecological resources while have carefully paid attention to saving the resources, the water scene treatment, fully utilizing the local architectural materials, and making use of the difference in the natural temperature to prevent cold and heat, which has reflected the ecological view attaching importance on partial ecological balance. The dwelling modalities are rich but not miscellaneous, skillful but not factitious because the numerous villagers who created them are accustomed to cultivation and conform to the rule of natural changes. The villagers always attach great importance on the harmony in contrast, the rhyme in gradual change, leading to a strong aesthetic sentiment of rural life with the characteristics as follows:

– Beauty in nature. The Chinese vernacular dwelling is always located at the places near mountains or waters; in the full sunshine or dark shadows; under bright sky

The vernacular dwelling of Shaoxing, Zhejiang Province.

Huizhou vernacular dwelling.

The chicken-leg wood dwelling.

The dwelling located in the Shade and faced to the sun while with hills behind and water in front.

The prosody of the horse-head wall.

or in dense forest . Beauty in nature has another enlightening meaning, that is: the man-made beauty in the Chinese vernacular dwelling is a kind of "meaning modality".

The vernacular dwelling's appearance, color, sense of reality, light and shadow, etc. closely relate to the function, material and structure of the civilian housing, for example, the horse-head wall for fireproofing, door awning for keeping out rain, the ridge tile for stopping up crack. The components and the decorates of Chinese civilian housing modality adhered to the practical need at the very beginning. Therefore they are unparalleled by those affected ones for their simple and crude beauty showing their specific original, natural, organic and simple character.

– Organic in random, disordered in appearance but implying rule in actuality. The most significant component of all kinds of civilian housing modalities is architectural material. Most rural houses adopt the local materials such as wood on the mountain, soil on the plain, rock on the shoal and grass on the field, which makes each house seem like growing on the land, and become an organic whole

The *Wufeng* Building in Western Fujian Province.

with the natural environment. They may be built alongside the mountain, suspend or support when it requires, which can be fully demonstrated by *Ganlan* wood building. As to the distribution of the housing settlement, it may distribute along the river way if near the river, with the lie of mountain when beside a mountain,

concentrate if on plains while scatter if not on plains, which seems disordered, though, contains the rule of "follow the nature".

– Harmonious but remaining differences. It is especially suitable for the modality requirements of the dwelling environment. The vernacular dwellings in a region mostly have the similar material, structure and composition of space and flat, forming the same color, sense of reality, appearance and even architectural "symbol", which indicates the tendency towards coherence of the civilian housing. But such kind of coherence tendency doesn't mean being totally the same; in fact, there are rich differences in the similar appearance, which can mainly be demonstrated by the combining arrangements of image elements and the subtle changes of the techniques. It displays the specific characters under the whole harmony of Chinese traditional culture and art, with a strengthening recognizability and high appreciation value.

Compared to urban architecture like palace, temple or mansion of high official and scholar, the rural local-style dwellings, together with such folk customs as slang and ditties, national dresses, local conditions, folk stories and even *Da A Fu*, cloth tigers, paper-cuts and "sugarcoated haws on a stick", constitute the so-called popular culture, which emerges, multiplies and develops in the grass-root rural or urban society with its strong vitality. It is created, enjoyed and passed on by the mass, and is close to their life.

The vernacular dwellings with the same structure but different in details.

It isn't exaggerated to say that the Chinese local-style dwellings contain the industriousness, wisdom and ideals of most Chinese people, reflecting the history of Chinese nationality. Among the Chinese traditional architectures, there are architectures as magnificent as imperial palaces, mansions, and the ones as elegant as gardens, academies and temples as well, the roots of which – from the mental software to the material hardware – are all unexceptionally based on the vernacular dwellings which possess traditional cultural charm.

by Shan Deqi

1 Huizhou Dwelling in Green Hills and Blue Waters

– A Talk on Huizhou Dwelling in the South of Anhui Province

◇ Huizhou in Hills and Waters – Hongcun:A Village of Rivers and Lakes

◇ Black and White Huizhou – A Land of Peach Blossoms: Xidi

◇ Imaginary and Real Huizhou – Patio and Horse-Head Wall

◇ Huizhou Fond of Books and Traditional Ethics – Colleges and Memorial Archways

◇ Huizhou's Techniques and Arts – "Carving of Three Kinds" and Gardens

◇ Huizhou's Merchants and Confucian Intellectuals – Business and Culture Supplement Each Other

Opening the map of China, we can find a well preserved area with a splendid culture and a long history, situated on the bank of the Xin'an River at the foot of the Huangshan Mountains in the south of Anhui Province. It is Huizhou.

Today's Huizhou is not an administrative division but a cultural circle of Chinese traditional national culture, including 5 counties in Anhui Province: Shexian, Xiuning, Qimen, Jixi and Yuxian, and a county in Jiangxi Province:Wuyuan.

The Huizhou Area registered a history of closely 2,000 years. Advanced economy and technology, brilliant arts and culture were developed there. The Cheng and Zhu Confucian School, Xin'an Painting School and four famous teams of Anhui Opera originated from there too. Additionally, this area produced *xuan* paper, Chinese ink-stick with Huizhou style and Shexian ink-stone. However, the something most well known to the people and with the most distinguishing feature in Huizhou is not other than the buildings with Huizhou style. Today, Huizhou's buildings have become precious heritages being deeply researched by domestic and foreign researchers on architecture.

16

Huizhou in Hills and Waters
– Hongcun: A Village of Rivers and Lakes

Huizhou are seized of green hills and clear waters, where the landscape is like a picture. The Huizhou dwellings adapted to the characters of hills and waters there and gave full play to them. The villages at Huizhou paid much attention to integrated planning, selecting location skillfully, geomantic omen and perfect structure. The buildings at Huizhou were usually located in the shade but faced to the sun, situated at the foot of a hill for using the water sufficiently and suiting measures to local conditions – if on plains, concentrated on a place and if not on plains, distributed dispersedly. The model of these villages is Hongcun, a village of rivers and waters, one of the world cultural heritages.

Hongcun is located at the north of Yixian, northward against Leigang Hill and southward to the Yangjian River. This position is just required by geomantic omen: "to be located in the shade but to face to the sun" and "with hills behind and water in front". The most distinguishing feature of Hongcun is artificial water channels distributed all over the village.

Hongcun began to be set up in the first year of the Shaoxing period of the Southern Song Dynasty (1131), but the construction of channels on a large scale began in the early Ming Dynasty. At that time, the villagers introduced the streamlets into the village, and dug channels with a length of over 300 meters, which flowed through the yards of every household at the village, and finally converged on a pond like a crescent moon in the front of the clan ancestral hall, built at the center of the village. 150 years afterward, the villagers opened a large pond – South Lake with a superficies of over 100 *mu* at the south of the village. In the 400 years from then on, this perfect structure of channels has been still reserved by Hongcun villagers and used by them in their ordinary life.

The entrance of the channel system is situated at a relatively high land, where the villagers built a dam with stone and installed a water gate to raise the water level. The water gate is the entrance of channels as well as the head of the channel system.

Hongcun with hills behind and water in front.

The center of Hongcun – the Moon Lake.

The general channels are 60 cm wide and 1 m deep, crossing circuitously through the lanes of the village, from the northwest to the southeast extending in all directions. A poet in the Ming Dynasty described: "In every dooryard flows a limpid streamlet". Lastly, all channels rush down into the village's center – the Moon Pond, whose north part is straight and south curved, like a new moon. Like a blood circulation system, the channel system stimulates the spiritual and material life of the village. On the one hand, the channel system plays a role of washing, fire protection, drainage and adjustment of temperature and humidity; on the other hand, together with the flagging, gardens and yards, squares and arches over gateway, it has become a changeable sight with distinguishing features and a public place for villagers' rest and social intercourse. Walking at Hongcun, we can see loquacious waters reflect mottle white walls and black tiles, green hills and blue sky; simple and unsophisticated flaggings connect profound courtyards, pavilions, terraces and open halls. In the South Lake at the south of village, we can see osier willows in spring, lotus flowers in summer, red leaves in autumn and white snow in winter – the sight in each season gives full play to its strong points. The channels not only link every house but also are introduced into the dooryard to form a small pond with its own feature. The water brings natural spirit to every house.

Water gate – channels – the Moon Pond – the South Lake, together with the small pond at every yard, compose an integrated water system and become the spirit of the village. The waters and hills, the streets, the lanes and the buildings, as well as villagers' life and culture form an integrated organism. The enlightenment from them is that the human beings can co-exist harmoniously with nature, utilize and protect the nature; nature is not only the object of human being's use and transformation, but also an indiscerptible part of human being's ordinary life.

Black and White Huizhou – A Land of Peach Blossoms: Xidi

The strongest characteristics of building groups at Huizhou are: the points, lines and surfaces composed of black tiles and white walls and the organic combination of black, white and gray colors, which constitute a Chinese ink-and-wash painting foiled in green hills and blue waters, elegant and refined. Originally, white walls of Huizhou dwellings were not for decoration but an ecological choice at that time, because whitewashed walls can protect against moisture and reflect sunshine. Afterward, with the development of culture, especially influenced by the Huangshan Mountains Painting School, the beauty of white and black colors has been more and more approbated by the people. Huizhou's developed culture and a number of intellectuals' quiet and simple but elegant aesthetic sentiment may be another cause of the popularization of black tiles and white walls.

Xidi Village is called "a residence at the land of peach blossoms", 8 kilometers to the east of Yi county town. The whole village keeps an integrated village structure and environment.

Xidi Village is a place where the Hu clan lives in compact communities. Streets and lanes in the village are zigzag, deep and changeful, with a delightful and cordial

A bird's-eye view of whole Xidi Village

constructive scale. They are ways for communication as well as places for villagers' intercourse. Everywhere can be found high or low "horse-head walls", door-visor with refined carving, arches and arch-doorways (*A doorway with an arch form, whose upper part is half-round, built by bricks.*), varied and vivid lattice windows and point-like windows (*The windows of this kind are very small, like point.*). Streets and lanes link gardens and yards, the later link patios, with a changeable and flowing special rhythm. Besides ordinary dwellings there are tall and upright ancestral halls, buildings for young ladies' living and memorial archways. Trees, streamlets and fields surround the village. Every building has sloping roofs towards different directions and corresponding horse-head walls which form black surfaces and lines foiled by the huge white walls. Zigzag streets, different directions of buildings and different height, storey and dimensions constitute a building style with organic changes; nevertheless, building materials and basic combinatorial mode are very accordant, so a sight of dwelling groups with both

19

A partial survey of Xidi, in which we can see the organic structure of black and white points, lines and surfaces.

20

a highly unified style and a lot of diversification come into being.

Of course, building's indoor colors are much more richer than its appearance. Usually, luxurious houses use red girders and pillars, the woodcarvings at important parts of which are decorated by golden powder; but generally intellectuals' families preferred doors, windows and furniture painted by varnish, with their original color of wood being left.

In fact, Huizhou dwellings did not copy existent colors in nature, but made a clear contrast against blue hills and green waters. and they are very harmonious with the colors of sky, land, hills and waters.

Imaginary and Real Huizhou – Patio and Horse-Head Wall

The traditional Huizhou dwellings were very mature in the Ming Dynasty. The most typical model was the courtyard house (four channels join inside the courtyard). Huizhou dwelling is a closed system, the external part is large and tall solid walls to guard against thefts only with some small windows for aeration. A number of Huizhou dwellings were intensively built, only separated by fireproof walls, which can curtain off fire and avoid fire's spread. Because

An inner patio under rain of a dwelling, built in the Ming Dynasty at Chengkan Village, a typical model of "four channels join inside the courtyard", tall and narrow patio shows a deep and remote artistic conception.

these walls have horse-head-like upper corners, they are called horse-head wall. The closed appearance of Huizhou dwelling is the "real" aspect; but in the inside of the dwelling the constructors used patios to communicate with nature. Patios of varied kinds distributed among large stretches of buildings. In the patios, bonsais flourish and the living atmosphere pervades – it is the "imaginary" aspect. Just in the combination of "imaginary" and "real", Huizhou dwelling arrived a realm in which art and life are perfectly unified.

Huizhou dwellings are very different from the quadrangles in the north of China. It is a product through the combination of wood storied building with railings and the quadrangle in the north of China. The courtyard house with Huizhou style is fundamentally storied building, the quadrangles only with one floor in the north of China are very rare in Huizhou area. Even if in a one-storey building, a wood floor was paved and an airflow interlayer was installed for removing humidity. In fact, Huizhou's houses built in the Ming Dynasty were storied

A group of horse-head walls with rich variety.

buildings, the principal activities of life were on the second floor, so the proportion between the first and the second floors was 1:2. But Huizhou's houses built in the Qing Dynasty accepted some features of northern quadrangles – residents' activities were basically at the first floor, then the proportion between the storeys turned 2:1. Nevertheless, the features of nest-like house were still kept: opening the central hall completely and linking it with the patio for better aeration. The proportion of patio is also different from the dimension of northern quadrangle's patio: tall and narrow for protection against the sunshine in summer, making the air upflowing. This kind of patio suits the hot climate in summer. The building structure also combined two wood structures: northern form of "raising beam" (*A form of wood structure in Chinese ancient buildings, the beam is put on the pillar and other beam put on this beam.*) and southern form of "mortise and quoin connecting" (*Another form of wood structure in Chinese ancient buildings, beam and pillar are connected by mortise and quoin.*), which are respectively used in main hall and in bed-rooms of

The door of Huizhou dwelling.

22

the same house. The gate of Huizhou dwelling also combines the features of southern stockaded village's gate and northern house's gate. The memorial archways and archway-like gates at Huizhou are typical examples.

Huizhou Fond of Books and Traditional Ethics – Colleges and Memorial Archways

From old times, culture and education at Huizhou developed very well. The Confucian Moral (*Li*) School of the Song and Ming dynasties had a far and deep influence upon Huizhou. Zhu Xi (1130-1200), a representative of the Confucian Moral School in the Southern Song Dynasty was born in Huizhou and gave lectures there. "Xin'an was abundant in famous intellectuals". "Even at a small village only with 10 households, nobody neglects cultivation and learning". Handing down books and courtesy to posterity is a tradition of Huizhou people. The reflection of this tradition in buildings at Huizhou resulted in many colleges, old-style private schools, ancestral halls and memorial archways.

There are a lot of old-style private schools and colleges. The famous ones are the South Lake College on the bank of the South Lake of Hongcun, Ziyang College and Zhushan College, etc. There were 52 colleges and 462 old-style private schools among the population of 560 thousand in Huizhou area in the Ming Dynasty. A great number of Huizhou natives secured official positions through imperial examinations. Many high-ranking officials and great intellectuals with reputation and power in the court and society were from Huizhou.

Huizhou paid much attention to the traditional ethics, which was also reflected by the construction of a great number of ancestral halls and memorial archways. An ancestral hall was the center of a clan. There were many clan settlments in

Huizhou so that Huizhou was very abundant in ancestral halls with very high rank. For example, the *Baolun* Pavilion at the backyard of Luo clan ancestral hall in Chengkan Village, was built in the Wanli period of the Ming Dynasty (1573-1619) and composed of 11 rooms, 29 meters wide and 10 meters deep, the architectural components full of decorations, among which the colored drawing on the beam in the bed-hall is a unusual treasure of folk colored drawing in China. *Jing'ai* Hall in the Hu clan ancestral temple at Xidi Village has two yards and three halls, with a commodious and solemn space, large and tall columns and beams, refined and splendid carvings and decorations. Like other ancestral halls, the position, dimension and superficies of these two buildings are highest in the villages. Ancestral halls in Huizhou's villages were the center of buildings as well as the spiritual center of villagers. Ancestor worship ceremony of a clan, important decision-making, rewards and punishment of all kinds were held

The South Lake College on the bank of the South Lake at Hongcun.

The inner sight of the *Jing'ai* Hall in the Hu clan ancestral temple at Xidi Village.

24

there. Today, ancestral halls at Huizhou's old villages have become a particular sight.

Memorial archways maintained the feudal code of ethics between clans and emperors. Huizhou's memorial archways are the first both in quantity and

Memorial archways at the entrance of Xidi Village.

A group of memorial archways at Tangyue Village.

in quality in all China. Only at Shexian, there are 94 memorial archways, among which are 34 memorial archways in honor of women's chastity. The memorial archways at Huizhou played an agile and changeful role: being a gate, indicating entrance or dividing up spaces. The memorial archway at the entrance of Xidi Village with 3 interspaces, 4 columns and 5 beams, 13

meters high, is the highest-rank memorial archway, which was granted by Emperor Wanli of the Ming Dynasty to Hu Wenguang, the governor of Jiozhou prefecture. The largest group of memorial archways are located at Tangyue, where 7 memorial archways stand silently in the fields with flourishing rape flowers. Their large scale, refined carvings and inscriptions with far and deep meanings manifest some families' history of honor and vicissitudes of life.

Inner sight of a building with wood carving at Lu Village.

Huizhou's Techniques and Arts – "Carving of Three Kinds" and Gardens

Huizhou's "Three Kinds of Carving" (wood, brick and stone carvings) are famous for their consummate techniques in all China. Especially, these carvings can be combined with indoor and outdoor components and decorations of the building, adding luster to the building and outstanding themselves. Building's door-visors, beam-heads, lattice windows, partition boards are refinedly made, exquisite beyond compare.

Huizhou's woodcarving is not daubed with colored paint but Chinese wood oil. The most precious woodcarvings used gingko and nanmu, which can show well the nobility and natural beauty of wood grain, furthermore refrain the negative influence of paint on woodcarving's details.

The material used in stone carving is the rock, called "Yixian Blue Stone". The stone carving was used in gates of

Lattice windows made of stone carving of a dwelling at Xidi Village.

Huizhou dwellings and memorial archways. The most surprised thing is the lattice window made of one-piece stone, with designs of proper density and a form combining hardiness with softness.

Huizhou's brick carving is made of blue brick with hard and exquisite quality, abundant at Huizhou. This carving is widely used in bars, gate-slipcover and lintels, constituting an important part of the buildings with Huizhou style.

As an important representative of Huizhou architecture, the garden with Huizhou style is characterized by bonsai and pond with Huizhou style. They are distributed at front part and back part of common people's houses, contacting closely with their ordinary life. *Tangan*

Brick carving on the gate of *Qingyi* Hall at Tangyue Village.

26

Tangan Garden at Tangmo Village.

Garden at Tangmo Village of Yixian County is a famous garden with Huizhou style, called "Small West Lake", built by Huizhou merchant Xu for his mother to get some idea of the landscape of the West Lake in Hangzhou. This garden was small and exquisite, drawing the architectural technique of Jiangsu and Zhejiang's gardens. The water-yard in Li Shuming house at Hongcun Village was situated back of the main room, out of the vestibule and extending to the small pond; the "arm-chair for beauties" (*An arm-chair, made of wood, generally used at garden; seated on it*

The water-yard in Wang Shunfeng's house at Hongcun Village.

ladies look more beautiful, so has this name.) and stone balusters on which put bonsai with Huizhou style, as well as lattice windows made of burnished bricks on the whitewashed walls, are all full of local and rural smell.

Huizhou's Merchants and Confucian Intellectuals – Business and Culture Supplement Each Other

The highly developed architectural culture at Huizhou isn't an occasional phenomenon; the most

important inner cause is the rise of Huizhou merchants with Confucian style. Being different from the merchants from Shanxi Province, merchants of Huizhou had an extroverted character because they came from a region where land is limited whereas the population is great, which forced them to leave their homeland to do business. Well cultured and educated, merchants of Huizhou were sharp-sighted, faithful, good at business, and understood that "becoming rich for developing Confucianism and being official for protecting business". So, they were very successful both in business and in officialdom. They engaged in salt, tea, pawn and publication businesses. The fortune was concentrated more and more in their hand. The stable economic foundation gave an impetus to culture's development and in turn, progressive culture

The Old Street at Tunxi has a commercial history of more than 100 years, and is still an important commercial district of today's Tunxi.

28

The patio in *Chengzhi* Hall at Hongcun Village, the wood carving painted by golden powder looks refined and magnificent.

Baolun Pavilion at Chengkan Village.

promoted Huizhou merchants' opening spirit in external intercourse and made economy more prosperous.

A large amount of Huizhou dwellings were built depending on Huizhou merchants' solid economic power. Influenced by Huizhou merchants' cultural quality, these buildings are refined but not vulgar nor extravagant. Ancestral halls, memorial archways and colleges – those buildings with most Huizhou characteristics could sufficiently develop only relying on Huizhou merchants' multiple identities – merchant, intellectual and official. Xu Guo (*Xu Guo was from Shexian county.*) Memorial Archway was built in commemoration of the minister and grand secretary Xu Guo's meritorious service in the Ming Dynasty, with the approval of the emperor. Other typical buildings of this kind include *Baolun* Pavilion at Chengkan Village, South Lake College at Hongcun Village, and many other Huizhou merchants' houses. All of them were built not only on the base of their fortune, but a result of all-round prosperity of economy, patriarchal clan system, culture and arts.

by Yuan Mu

2 *Ganlan* Wood House and Storm-Tossed Bridge
– A Visit to Northern Guangxi Mountain Villages

As China's territory is vast, the architectural forms of various folk houses are extremely splendid and colorful. The *ganlan* wood houses are distributed mainly over the vast land of northern part of Guangxi, eastern part of Guizhou Province, western part of Hunan, where they are densely situated or scatter in the mountains. The *ganlan* wood house along with the stockaded village gate, *lusheng* (a reed-pipe wind instrument) level ground and the storm-tossed bridge has become the home for the existence of many minority nationalities like *Miao, Dong, Zhuang, Yao* nationalities, etc.

Ganlan can also be referred as *Malan*. In the language of the Zhuang nationality *Ganlan* means "home", "house". *Ganlan*'s evolution and development witnessed a history of several thousand years. *Ganlan* wood houses preserved living traditions and national coquette.

A Tour to Wood-House Village

The shapes of the wood-house villages in the northern Gaungxi hilly areas were in thousands of postures which originated from the distribution pattern of folk houses,

The *Ganlan* wood building of Ping'an Village, Longsheng County.

such as crossing the stream, beside the foothills, or around a valley. The wood-house village usually has a village gate (the Dong nationality's wood-house village often has storm-tossed bridges besides village gate) while some wood-house villages might have several gates.

The Longji thirteen villages of Multinational Autonomous County of one hundred km away from Guilin city and 1000 meters above sea level, is known as symbol of the world terraced fields, where the terraced fields are both imposing and winding. The Zhuang nationality had to face the adverse circumstances, for instance, the Ping'an Village is a village situated at the highest sea level among the thirteen villages. The largest terraced field here does not exceed one *mu* (1 *mu*=0.0667 hectares).

Upon the Ping'an Village, all families without exception are linked by a twist and precipitous mountain road. The wood buildings of the same color with slope roofs are braced on the ground of the slopes. Some timber buildings are five to six meters above the ground, among which spread plots of terraced fields. A cluster of timber houses should be built in line with the topography while the village should be adjacent to farming land so as to be convenient to intensive cultivations. Due to the historical changes, among many villages of the Dong Autonomous County of Sanjiang, there are cases that several villages are often adjacent to each other or even link with each other. The three villages of Linxi can be cited as a good example. Among the three villages the Huangchao Village is one occupying a commanding height. Entering the village through slope flights of steps people should pass through a village gate

Huangle Village, Longsheng County.

in a shape of pavilion. The plane of the village is rectangular. The village gate, drum tower, water pool and small drum tower are built in proper sequence. They are neatly arranged.

The terraces in Longji.

The Yan Village is a timber-building village situated at a riverside and near a brook. To enter the village from the storm-tossed bridge one should pass the wandering footpath to the village gate. The height mark is slightly higher than the river channel, which has given rise to a distinctive village gate of the Yan Village – its entrance is at the bridge gallery of the drum tower. Ascending from the footpath along the river channel, and one can enter into the village. The small storm-tossed bridge in front of the Yan Village is naturally connected the Liang Village which also has an independent village gate and drum tower. The three villages are dispersed on the three points in different styles.

32

The Zuolong Village of the Dulong Township is surrounded by waters in three directions while another direction faces a mountain slope. The appearance of the village is just like a sleeping dragon. This is only a small village composed of forty-odd families. Because of the narrow footpath and the scattered wood houses even the animals should climb the steps, but there are still the

ZuoLong Village, just like a lying dragon.

The entrance to the Yan Village below the gallery.

drum tower, family temples and village gates among clusters of wood houses.

Singing in Antiphonal Style at the Chengyang Bridge

On the festive occasions the fellow villagers of Dong nationality bringing along the old and young were jubilant to flock to the Chengyang Bridge from all directions. The young boys and girls of the Dong Nationality dressed in their holiday best, were

The full view of Chengyang Bridge

33

The youth of Dong nationality singing in antiphonal style on Chengyang Bridge.

setting off crackers while dancing the " *Cai Tang*" dance accompanied with reed-pipe wind instrument. People were gathering at the head of the Chengyang Bridge. The passageway was blockaded with the stable fences made of green bamboo by the youngsters and girls. On the days of jubilation or during the festive activities all guests coming here to visit their relatives and friends were declined to enter the village. The youngsters and girls neither check your passes nor ask for money, but they only want to sing in antiphonal style with you. Please listen to the song of "*blocking the way*".

> *Never seen such a brilliant Sunlight,*
> *Never seen such colorful flowers,*
> *The appearances of the Dong nationally,*
> *Have changed a lot,*
> *Because the guests coming from afar today...*

Just like the storm-tossed bridge of the Dong nationality the songs of them are characteristic of cordiality, harmony, simplicity and grace. When the guests could correct link the song they would be permitted to enter the village through the bridge and well received. Such a kind of jubilant occasion could be easily found in the Dong villages or Dong townships. But the Chengyang Bridge is one of the "state

major units of historical relics under protection". Therefore singing in antiphonal style on Chengyang Bridge has a special cultural flavour.

The Chengyang Bridge was built by the people of the eight Dong villages such as Chengyang Village, Ma'an Village, etc. headed by five old Dong men, who mobilized the village to offer the timbers or contribute their labor while tilling the

The Chengyang Bridge, completely constructed by wood.

land. The best stonemasons and carpenters were invited here to construct. It took 12 years to accomplish the construction of the Chengyang Bridge.

Situated at Linxi Township of Sanjiang County of the Northern Guangxi, the Chengyang Bridge is across the Linxi River. It is 64 meters in length, 3 meters in width and more than 10 meters in height. It is a four-arched bridge with five piers. Each arch of main girders of bridge was built in two layers with seven China firs that about half meter in diameter, 30 meters in length. Then planks would be paved, columns erected, beams put up. At last, the roof would be constructed and covered with tiles. Along both sides of bridge installed the banisters. In the Linxi township there are about 15 storm-tossed bridges. Its local name is "floral bridge". People are overwhelmed with the fact that the whole bridge fully depend upon its through-

The Storm-tossed bridge of Dong nationality with the pavilion with *xieshan*-style roof.

The Batuan storm-tossed bridge of Dong nationality.

jointed frame and corbel, without any iron nails and screws.

Every village of Dong nationality of the Northern Guangxi has its own bridge which is different from others in the style. Some are composed of three pavilions; some four pavilions; some, five pavilions; some are covered with rectangle or hexagonal spires, two to five layers of eaves; some are with *Xieshan*-style roofs. The more interesting is that the storm-tossed bridges at the Town Ba Tuan have double decks. The upper deck is for people to walk on while the lower deck for draught animals.

The storm-tossed bridge is just entrance of a village, which is a passage linking the two banks of the rivers and streams. It is the only way to enter the village as well as the symbol of a village.

Drum Tower and *Lusheng* Column

The drum tower in every Dong Village (some Dong villages have two or more drum towers) can make an appropriate comparison with the storm-tossed bridge. The drum tower strikingly stands on the

The facade of the drum tower in Yan Village.

The nine-layer *xieshan*-style roof of the Mapang drum tower.

drum tower level ground. It is also the fine products of Dong architectural art.

The drum tower can be divided into two parts: the lower part like pavilion while the upper part like a pagoda. The lower part is supported by eight columns. The four outside columns are used for supporting the pavilion eaves while the inside columns of China firs are used for supporting the beams. The upper part is constructed with multiple eaves and corbel brackets which can be distinguished into rectangle, hexagon or octagonal eaves. Multiple eaves can be five layers or seven layers, or even nine layers or eleven layers.

The steeple of the drum tower is often installed with precious bottle gourd and millennium crane that represents good luck. The ground inside of the drum tower is usually paved with stone and built with fire

The Totem *Lusheng* Column of Miao nationality.

pit and installed with seats along the walls, which has a seating capacity of 100-200 people. As a matter of fact, the drum in the tower is only a hollow-out huge wood covered with the cattle hides at both ends. The drum tower is a place where the villagers discuss public business or work out regulations or rules for township administration. Secondly drum beating can also sound the alarm for bandits or robbers. The beating is the signal for gathering and joint actions.

The center of the Dong village is the drum tower while the center of the Miao village is the *Lusheng* column, which is a vertical huge China fir decorated with ox horns, dragons, phoenixes and broadsword. Its top is a phoenix shape. The *Lusheng* column stands on the *Lusheng* level (ground surrounding the *Lusheng* column), there are designs made of cobblestones on the ground. The *Lusheng* column is the totem of Miao Nationality.

37

Ganlan Wood Houses

Guangxi Zhuang Nationality Autonomous Region is a wooded and hilly land with damp and hot weather as well as abundant rainfall, while there are poisonous snakes and beasts of prey in the mountain areas. Therefore the vernacular dwellings are mainly the *Ganlan* wood houses in the northern hilly areas of Guangxi.

The *ganlan* houses made of bamboo or wood frame had been gradually perfected by the ancestors. People lived on the second floor while the first floor without walls was mainly used for storage of miscellaneous things or served as pigsties or sheepfolds.

The outer surface of the Liao Family wood building.

38

The *ganlan* wood houses are usually based upon a rectangular plane of " three rooms with four trusses". (*The building of "three rooms with four trusses is China's traditional architecture having three rooms in façade while there are four lines of rafter on the roof truss*)

In line with different conditions such as family population, topography of building foundation and its relationship with roads, the building planes in the shape of "L", " 凸 "and " 凹 " were derived; moreover, the buildings are usually constructed on the slopes of mountain, therefore, two-storeyed or three-storeyed rectangular units are more popular in order to economize the land. The rectangle plane often contains staggered floor or skip-floor. The wood houses in the Dong Autonomous County of Sanjiang are mainly topped with four-sloped roofs but those of the Miao village in the Miao Autonomous County of Rongshui are topped with two-sloped roofs. The main materials of roofs are grey tiles, while the wood houses in wooded mountains may use the shingles. The protection walls with small windows are also constructed with planks. The bay of a small wood house in the northern part of Guangxi ranges from three to five meters, which mainly depends on the size of the China firs. The

The suspending pillars and protruding beams of the *Ganlan* wood building.

The wood structure with no roof beams and the technology
of mortise and tenon of the wood building in Yan Village.

The wood structure of the Meng Village wood building under construction.

The suspending pillar of the wood building.

whole wood building is connected with mortise and tenon but not the iron articles.

At the bottom the wood columns are usually placed on the building foundation while putting stone blocks under the columns. The wood system bears the force as a whole, therefore even if one column was destroyed or the stone-block under a column was moved away the monolithic wood house won't move an inch. The advantages of such a construction are as follows: In the mountain areas it is difficult to find the flat foundations for construction; readjustment of length of wood column tallying with the height of ground level could free from the limitation of the height of building foundation. In line with necessities, the peripheral wood wall bodies for protection may be totally closed; or closed with small windows; or opened with balcony railing. The extension or connection of the wood houses would be more convenient. Such a construction is also beneficial to discharge rainfalls and resist

The fire pit in a wood building in Ping'an Village.

earthquakes.

It is worthy of noting that the *ganlan* wood houses in the northern part of Guangxi are characterized by two peculiar elements: hanging pillar and overhanging eaves. In order to increase the floorage of a wood house on the limited land, the stretching-out technology is used on every floor; which requires the brackets on the transverse beams to carry the load of the upper stretching-out pillars, forming a through-jointed frame through the way of mortise and tenon. The ends of the pillars extend, forming the hanging pillars.

The head of the hanging pillar has always been polished and carved to form the shape of lotus or lanterns, which are similar to the festoon decoration on the door of the courtyard and house in Beijing. Popular use of cantilever beams under the eaves is mainly for the rainy and hot climate in south China. Therefore, the wood house often has long plancier pieces which can be as long as 1.5 meters. The vertical props under the eaves are outriggers with purloins. The larger plancier pieces always have two or three layers of outrigger. Although the total wood house is not carved with exquisite sculpture, its modeling is light and graceful through well arrangement of through-jointed frame, hanging posts, balconies, cantilever beams together with stagger floor and overlap joints.

Fire Pit – the Holy Place in the Wood House

Every family of the northern part of Guangxi Zhuang Nationality Autonomous Region has built a fire pit in the middle of the room on the second floor of the

ganlan wood house, while big wood building may have two or three fire pits.

The fire pit is a one-square-meter opening for fire burning on the floor with a subsided square *dou* (a measure for grain shaped like a cup), the timbers bearing the heavy load of fire pit are placed on the beams. The fire pit bottom is brimmed with wood sheeting and fireproof earth.

The youths and girls of Zhuang nationality singing in antiphonal style.

The wood house would be filled with smoke when the charcoal is burning in the fire pit. With the elapse of time, the walls and ceilings of the houses will be stuck with the soot, which would darken the interior space of the wood house. But the villagers said that the soot would serve as damp-proof and preservative agents.

In a family the fire pit is of great significance, in addition to its cooking functions, it is the public contact place for family getting-together, guest reception and leisure chat and so on. The fire in the fire pit will never extinct from time to time. The fire pit is also a holly place. The casual action of leaping over the fire pit is regarded as an irreverent behavior. The Zhuang villages in the Long Sheng County always sang in antiphonal style around the fire pits.

A pile of fire, a pot, a cup of tea and a song constitute the most popular local life of the Zhuang nationality and give the fire pit a cultural connotation. Here, architectural leisure life integrates with national atmosphere.

by Shan Deqi

3 The City along Jade Water and Full of Historical Charm
– A Tour of Ancient Lijiang Streets

◇ Ancient City Shaped in Thousand -Year Vicissitudes
◇ A City Surrounded by Spring Water
◇ Trace the Vernacular Dwellings Through Three Terrace Houses with One Screen Wall

Lijiang lies in the northwest of Yunnan Province. It is being known to more and more people. There are the well kept ancient city and vernacular dwellings, the Yulong Snow Mountain, the mysterious Dongba culture and the sincere Nahsi People. The people there enjoy a natural and quiet life. There are many other scenic spots like the Tiger-leaping Gorge, Lugu Lake, Jade-peak Temple, etc. Lijiang is really an attractive resort and a place with Oriental charm in Southwest China.

Ancient City Shaped in Thousand-Year Vicissitudes

The ancient city is the most attractive thing for tourists forgetting return during their Lijiang Tour, while the ancient vernacular dwellings are the most attractive ones in the city.

The Da Yan Ancient Town, part of the Lijiang Ancient City is a small and beautiful town, which is something like Venice and Suzhou, while it has richer flavor of rural life than Venice and Suzhou. It has been integrated with scenic mountains and rivers and mingled with the scattered villages. The Lijiang Ancient City has witnessed the vestige and vicissitudes of the Nahsi nationality from generation to generation. So many stories of the historical legends handed down in the streets and lanes, in the imposing dwellings and courtyards, as well as in shops and workshops of the ancient

44

city. Therefore, the ancient city is a place for Nahsi people's living and cultural consumption. It is more valuable that the diligent and honest Nahsi people are still living in the vernacular dwellings spreading over all corners of the ancient city. Therefore, this is a "living" ancient city that has registered historical changes while following the modern times. Because of the above-mentioned distinguished features and special values, the Li Jiang Ancient City has been inscribed in the World Heritage List by the World Heritage Committee of the UNESCO in 1997.

The development of cities and towns is synchronous with the social and economic progress of the local areas. The Lijiang Ancient City, of course, has no exception. During the Sui and Tang Dynasties, the Nahsi nationality were called "Moshayi" who established tribal villages. Viewing from historical outlook of tribal village's development, these tribal villages were the source for the development of the Lijiang Ancient City. The vernacular dwellings at that time were the initial shape of the modern "Batten" houses. The commodity exchange and rural fair would naturally appear in a definite period of agricultural development. Thus, the market towns emerged as an embryonic form of modern cities and towns. The Dayandi of the Yu River Reaches can be regarded as the typical of the market town evolved from the ancient villages.

"Seven Stars with the Moon", the folk costume of Nahsi Nationality.

The Dayandi occupies the central position of the Lijiang scenic area and locates at bag bottom of upper reaches of Jinsha River, being surrounded by big mountains and Jinsha River as the natural city wall and city moat respectively. It is a place easy to be defended and control the whole area of River reaches. Kublai Khan the first emperor of the Yuan Dynasty (1260-1294 at reign) led the Mongolian troops to cross the Jinsha River. The military headquarters headed by Aliang Ahu, son of Kublai Khan was located at the Dayandi. Aliang Ahu started the construction of the ancient town Dayan through excavation of Jade River and West River, which laid the foundation for developing the town along the Jade River, West River and Middle River. This was the predecessor of the Lijiang Ancient City. Up to the Ming Dynasty at the reign of the Emperor Zhu Yuanzhang (reign from 1368-1398) the local headman

Mu was granted the title of county magistrate of Lijiang area. After headman Mu moved his government from Baisha to Dayan Town, he went in for large-scale construction of the ancient town that had become the hub of communication with the Sifang Street in the center. During the reign of Emperor Yongzheng, the local officials were replaced by the court officials who excavated the East River of the Jade River. Finally the Lijiang Ancient City with the river system of three rivers (West River, Middle River and East River) and the street and lane network was formed, the Sifang Street at the center.

45

A City Surrounded by Spring Water

The water is the soul of the ancient city while its beauty can not exist without the water.

The Helong Pond is the water-head of the Yu River in the City. The spring water gushes out from roots of

An overlook of the ancient city.

old chestnut-trees at the foot of the Elephant Mountain, forming a huge and mystical pond of debouchure. The spring water in the pond flows from the northwest of the ancient city to the Yulong Bridge, which has a dam with three channels for shunting the water. The water of Yu River is shunted into three streams: the East River, the Middle River and the West River which flow into the city. Henceforth, the water of Yu River which is the living source of the ancient city flows gently as a murmuring stream.

The water of the West River, Middle River and East River has been further shunted into numerous tributaries to every street of the ancient city. The city's free layout not sticking to one pattern is due to this favorable natural condition. The main streets of the city stand by the rivers while lanes are constructed along channels; the roads extended in line with the twists and turns of the channels, while sites of houses are well selected in accordance with the topography; it is marvelous to say that "every family can enjoy spring water and appreciate picturesque willow at windows". It is beyond doubts that tourists both at home and abroad called it "Suzhou on the Highland" or "the Oriental Venice".

Entering the city along the rivers or channels, the outline of the ancient city is clearly discernible. The water system will surly be accompanied by all kinds of bridge. The bridges of Lijiang city are full of charm. Only when looking for the Nahsi old men, women and children bustling with activities in the street and pondering over the Nahsi vernacular dwellings and their life could you understand the intimate relationship among water, bridge, building and the ancient city.

Stepping into the ancient city, you can find

The Sifang Street, the heart of the ancient town.

the roads paved with greenish marble lead the tourists to roam in the city. The greenish marble roads are different from the common roads paved with slabstones, the polished faces of the marble have shown colorful motifs, which are composed of pebbles in different colors. The marble is a kind of natural stone, which is called "5-color marble". All slates were extracted from the mountains of Lijiang basin. If you have a careful observation you may find the uneven faces of the marbles are full of black spots with different shades, which have written down the vestiges of human steps and horse-heels in several hundred years. In recent

Streams are the arteries of this beautiful town.

Various kinds of bridges in Lijiang ancient town.

days, more attention is paid to the southern silk route. Some argued that here was the trade passage and cultural corridor earlier than the Northwest silk route. Lijiang was one of the important posts (where former couriers changed horses or rested) on the ancient tea-horse road. In fact, the vestiges left by the caravans are the cultural imprint, a mark of cultural communications and integration.

The street fairs of the ancient city had formed general appearance of the city custom. The Sifang Street was the representation of the country fair of the ancient city. In ancient times it was just a primitive country fair and later on it had become an important place for tea-horse exchange on the ancient tea-horse route. Now street pedlars gathered here while people are dazzled by antiques and articles for daily use. The great landscape of the country fair are composed of opening tarpaulin canopies, big umbrella made of butter paper and the traditional pedlars. In the west part of fair gathered all kinds of ancient or old handcrafts while at the east part of fair, people are selling articles for daily use, such as pans, bowls, gourd ladle and basins and so on. The big pot cover can be used as straw hat while the copper gourd ladles and spoons are as bright as mirrors. The square for country fair has four streets radiating in four directions, i.e. Guangyi Street, July 1 Street, May 1 Street in

the east and Xinhua Street in the west; while each street has several lanes. Thus, an opening arrangement has been formed with the Sifang Street at center surrounded by shopping stores, hotels and restaurants. After careful observation you may find the streets of the Nahsi City are markedly different from those traditional streets arranged in the shape of Chinese character " 井 ". Other street markets also have their own characteristics. They are the extension and complementary of the Sifang Country Fair.

Trace the Vernacular Dwellings Through "Three Terrace Houses with One Screen Wall"

The Lijiang's vernacular dwellings are the cultural and living crystallization of the Nahsi people. These dwellings are characterized by simpleness, freshness and natural beauty and are expression of the continuance of the local culture as well as

Yulong Snow Mountain is the divine mountain in the hearts of the Nahsi people. The ancient town has a extremely close relationship with the mountain.

(*up*) The wood bridge in Dayan town.
(*down*) A part of Sifang Street.

(*up and down*) The old streets have recorded a lot of lyric times.

the combination and conflicts of pluralistic cultures. To appreciate the vernacular constructions of Lijiang is just like drinking a cup of old liquor or tasting a cup of cocktail wine.

Lijiang City with its own cultural and historical tradition has its own history of architectural development. The Lijiang vernacular dwellings have

The Xianwen Lane.

The stone slabs on the road have been polished by times.

50

The West River beside
traditional buildings.

developed from vernacular dwelling
models like "house in caves", "house
on the trees" and "batten seam house
of log construction" to those of "three
terrace houses with one screen wall"
and "quadrangle residential with 5
small yards" and "horse-mounted
house with lapped corner joints".

Obviously, the vernacular
dwellings of the Nahsi nationality in
Lijiang Area have undergone the
evolution from batten seam houses to
courtyard style of the Han nationality.

The batten seam house is the
primitive mode of the folk house of
the Nahsi nationality in the Lijiang
Area. This is a wood-structured
house, its walls are vertically and
horizontally built with barked timbers
while its roof is covered with planks.

Street and Shops.

The ancient city also welcomes modern people and has
many modern shops.

The building material can be obtained easily from the local environment while it is simple to master the art of batten seam house construction.

The original spatial mode of the batten seam house was only a yard which was gradually transformed into more regular amalgamated dwelling under the influence of foreign culture. Such a dwelling consisted of principal rooms, wing house (scripture hall), dress circle, bar straw house. The principal rooms are places used for family gathering, meetings, cooking and offering sacrifices to gods or ancestors. The wing house can also be called Buddhist religious scripture hall. It is usually a two-storied building. The second floor is bedrooms of Lama or room for worshiping Buddhist images while the rooms on the first floor are prepared for the bachelors or guests. The dress circle mainly serves as the bedrooms of the young maids. The second floor of gateway serves as the room for storage of straws while at both sides of the gate on the first floor are the cattle shed.

The gate of Musuo people's building usually faces the east or north. The yard is always rather big where the wedding or funeral ceremonies could be held here. The structure of principal room is quite complicated. In the back of the room is a sandwich structure for food stockpile and serving as the bedroom of the old people. The right side of the principal room is the living room for housewife; in one corner of principal room is the top of the kitchen range and on the corner of which is placed a shrine on which placed the god statue, sacrifices, and vase. Under the kitchen range is the fire pit. The right side of the fire pit is prepared for the hosts while the left side is reserved for guests. There are two big columns in the room, one is called left

A part of the traditional batten-seam house of the Nahsi people.

The traditional batten-seam house of the Nahsi people.

column or male column while the other is referred as right column or female column. The grown-up ceremony of men will be held at the side of left column while that of women will be held at the side of the right column. Obviously the form of the batten seam house are inseparable to living conditions and living way of the agricultural society of the Nahsi nationality, because people's daily life, natural environment and technologies will decide its structures and modes. Of course, the spatial structure of the building has close relationship with people's religious beliefs, marriage status as well as family structure. Here, the buildings are given more cultural colors and symbolic significance by the initial ideology of the minorities.

The traditional vernacular dwelling of the Nahsi people in Lijiang Area, however have absorbed more merits of courtyard building of the Hans on the bases of maintaining their good traditions.

In 1921 Mr. Locher, an American scholar came to Lijiang area and began to study the Dongba culture of the Nahsi people. He made friends with the local people. The Lijiang people warmly received him because they did not exclude the alien culture. Locher's research findings have played an important role in helping the people both at home and abroad to understand Li Jiang better.

The Nahsi ancesters adopted the open policy in culture. And for a long period of time, the Dayan ancient town was an important communication post on the Sichuan and Tibetan trade corridor while it objectively played the role of cultural corridor. Therefore the Nahsi people has a good tradition of worshiping the culture while being well versed in learning to absorb other progressive cultures. If you make a careful observation of Nahsi vernacular dwellings you may find the great influences of the tradition of the cultural integration on the art of folk house's construction. You can also find the architectural culture, forms and styles of the Nahsi, Han, Bai and Tibet nationalities in complete harmony.

There are many types of common Nahsi vernacular dwellings: Three Terrace Houses with One Screen Wall, Front and Back Courtyard, etc. Among them, the most basic and common dwelling of the Naxi nationality in Lijiang is the Three Terrace Houses with One Screen Wall. The three terrace houses are characterized by higher principal room, lower wing rooms with one screen wall, which is distinct of what is primary and what is secondary. The long plancier at the top had definite curve "face slope" so as to avoid heavy and rigid impression, while demonstrating its gentle and beautiful curves. The body of wall is appropriately tumbling in, which strengthened the impression of stability about the whole building. The surrounding walls are lower to the top. The ornamental perforated wood windows are installed at above the sills. Most of eaves are stretched-out to protect the plank from being wet by the rain; at the two ends of cross girders projecting from the gable is installed skirt board, which is called " fire-sealing gable". In order to make the house more beautiful, some buildings are installed with the banisters in shape of the covered way. Finally, in order to reduce the dull atmosphere caused by the abrupt change of Chinese overhang eaves fascia and the exposing gable post the art of vertical weatherboarding are ingeniously applied, which can either protect the cross girders, or increase the art beauty of the whole building. A harmonious appearance of a building full of changing beauty has taken its shape through reasonable arrangement of principal room and wing rooms, screen walls, wall body and festoon decoration. The vernacular dwelling of "three terrace houses with one screen wall" have shown the superb architectural skills of the Nahsi nationality.

The principal room of the Nahsi dwellings for the aged people usually faces the south and the wing rooms for younger generation on the east or west are slightly lower. The first floor is mainly for people's living while the second floor serves as warehouses. The courtyard is mainly paved with bricks or stones and beautified with flowers and grasses.

The front of the Nahsi building is usually attached with a gallery which is an integral part of the Nahsi building in Lijiang area. Now some room's functions for

The batten-seam house at the foot of Yulong Snow Mountain.

dinner or receiving guests are substituted by the gallery. The country fair has been high developed in the Dayan ancient city since ancient time while the Nahsi people are good merchants. Therefore the vernacular dwellings overlooking the street will be used as shop front by the house-owner.

As a matter of fact, the real, simple and natural life in the Nahsi vernacular dwellings has nurtured the moderate cultural mentality. Living in such a dwelling, you will feel the existence of the Nahsi culture.

by Wang Dong

4 Harmonious Combination of Chinese and Western Elements

– Catching the Architectural Novelty in the Homeland of the Overseas Chinese

◇ Towering Watchtower – Witness of Local History
◇ Row upon Row of Zigzag Arcade-houses
◇ Ancestral Temples Remain the Same Charisma

A mixture of Western pillar corridor and Chinese roof.

There, in Wuyi Region of Guangdong Province, exist a lot of civilian residential dwellings with obvious alien cultural elements and the style and decoration so different from Chinese traditional building style. When you look round, there are dwellings of Romanesque, Gothic, Byzantine styles, Islamic style and traditional Chinese style.

The watchtower dwelling group in a village.

In China, Wuyi Region is a well-known area inhabited by returned overseas Chinese and their relatives. From 1911 to 1949, a large number of Wuyi people went abroad for life. The statistics of 1999 indicated that there were 3.6 m Wuyi local people living abroad, scattering in more than 100 countries and regions all over the world. These returned overseas Chinese, when returned, not only brought huge sum of fortune, but also Western new ideas and philosophy, including Western architectural culture and technology, which promoted the combination of Chinese traditional architectural style and alien culture and produced today's regional features of the harmonious combination of Chinese and Western elements in the local civilian residential dwellings.

Wuyi is not an independent name but a popular name of five areas of Xinhui, Taishan, Enping, Kaiping and Heshan in Guangdong Province. Administratively, the above five areas all are under the jurisdiction of Jiangmen Municipality of Guangdong Province, now called "four cities and one district".

Towering Watchtower –Witness of Local History

In this area, the buildings which most impress the people and best reflect the regional features are the scattered watchtower-style residential dwellings in mountains and villages. Watchtower, by definition, is a tower-looking building, the main purpose of the building was to defend the village and prevent the bandits from attack and robbery. Once in emergence, all villagers could move into the tower for security. On the upper part of the tower, there was outlier corridor for the insiders to occupy a commanding position to fire at those attackers. Generally, those watchtowers are located in the rear or on both sides of the village, occupying the commanding position. At least there were 2 or 3 towers in each village, and at most 7 or 8 ones. A lot of watchtowers are still remaining in Wuyi region, with Kaiping owns most of the existing ones. According to the incomplete statistics, there are more than 1 400 towers in Kaiping in the year of 2 000.

The architectural style of watchtower originated rather early. In early Qing Dynasty, there already appeared such towers in villages round Kaiping. Up to the early 20th century, with the inflow of the large sum of overseas capital, the financial conditions of many relatives of overseas Chinese were greatly improved, for example, in Taishan County only, the overseas remittance reached as high as US$ 10 million before 1929, after 1929, it rocketed to US$30 million. At the same time, the public order in these overseas villages was from bad to worse. Those rich families were regarded as the "financial source" in the eyes of local bandits. The bandits were on a rampage in the villages, robbing and blackmailing. The local people had no way out but to organize to build towers to safeguard themselves. Today, the defensive function of the towers disappeared, but the towers remain to be the witness of the past history, creating a unique historical atmosphere, producing kind of sense of alien beauty, making another contribution to the regional resident dwellings.

The towers in Wuyi generally own 3 to 6 floors, a few of them 7 to 9 floors. Its plane basically takes the shape of square. The tower is divided into 3 parts: tower body, outlier floor and roof. The lower part is the body of the tower, which, for

The *Duanshi* Building in Taishan, graceful in shape and harmonious in proportion.

the purpose of defense, appears thick and strong with small windows and a lot of bullet holes. Limited by a series of military functions such as defense, the shape of tower body is very simple and distinctive, large piece of solid wall gives a strong sense of weight and closed system, but after all it was not the real tower for war, it was the place for local people to live in, hence it should also show to some degree the sense of beauty, their love of life, so that there appeared the delicate window frame above the windows. The upper part of the firm and strong body is the relative spacious part called outlier floor, where people could look out or launch counter-attack. Along the corridor there were bullet holes on the wall and the floor. Judged from the shape, the corners of some outlier floors appears tube-shaped,

The *Jingshoutian* Building in Kaiping County.

The exquisite lines on the gatecase.

others octagon-shaped, like "swallow net", a lot more to be the pillar-shaped European style. In addition to the military implication, the outlier corridors, we can find, also give the architectural implication in terms of aesthetics and ecology. Aesthetically, these corridors and the closed wall match each other so well that they produce the contrast between vacancy and reality. Ecologically, the open corridors are of benefit to ventilating, to the improvement of people's living environment in southern Guangdong Province, where the climate usually is moist and dump. The most magnificent part of such building is the housetop, which was mostly sitting on the square or polygon bases, forming beautiful skylines.

Judged from the building materials and styles, the watchtowers could be divided into three types: clay building, brick building and reinforced concrete building. Clay and brick were building materials of Chinese traditional resident dwellings, while the reinforced concrete was the material born under the influence of Western culture. These towers were mostly built in the 1920's or 30's of the last century. Those overseas owners, when absorbing the different building styles of different countries, built them with the then most advanced materials and technology. Those buildings fully displayed the merge and clash of cultures of East and West, ancient and contemporary. Which is specifically reflected in two aspects: one is that so many cultural factors, such as Chinese traditional style, ancient Greek and Romanesque styles, European Gothic style of Middle Ages and Islamic style, gathered in such small region; the other is that so many different architectural styles manifested in one building, forming a kind of "hors d'œuvres" in a compromising way.

In these overseas Chinese villages, another attractive resident dwelling is called "Lu". "Lu" is the elegant name of the resident dwelling for those well-to-do overseas Chinese families, to some degree like

The roof of the stone building is of a variant Byzantine style.

The miraculous combination of Chinese-style banister and Western-style Columns.

60

modern times villa. "Lu" usually has 2 or 3 floors, located in the environmentally elegant places of the village. The outlook design and structure of the building appeared liberal and flexible, suitable for people to inhabit. The outlook of "Lu" is very similar to that of the watchtower because of their building style and materials, but since "Lu" was rather low in floors, with more windows, the defensive function of the wall was naturally reduced, while life atmosphere increased. In addition, the traditional outlier corridor of towers was gradually changed into the concave spatial corridor, with a more reasonable spacious effect and ratio.

The combination of Chinese and Western architectural cultures is also embodied on the *Lu*-style building.

Row upon Row of Zigzag Arcade-houses

If the watchtowers could be said the typical representative of the resident dwelling in rural areas, the arcade-dwelling could be named the representative of the resident dwelling in towns of Wuyi region. Towns were usually the distributing center for commercial exchange and trade. Where there are towns, there are commercial activities. In the past, there were few specialized commercial facilities in large scale, mostly were buildings with the first stage used as store and the second stage used as living room, or with stores in front and dwelling in the back part. These arcade-dwellings combining business with dwelling became typical resident dwelling in the towns in southern

Guangdong Province.

Arcade-dwelling are common commercial buildings in the southern regions in China, they usually have 2 or 3 floors, the front part of the first floor is called pillar corridor. Pillar corridors of many buildings connected , thus the public pavement was formed. It is hot and rainy in south China, in order to let people stay away from sunlight or rain, the pavement was sheltered by the pillar corridors. With the prosperity of towns, a house was added on the pillar corridor to increase the building areas, in this way the earliest arcade dwelling came into being. The construction of arcade-dwelling made it convenient for the customers to do their shopping, and was beneficial to the marketing of commodities. Both customers and businessmen liked it very much. Arcade-dwelling, a product in the combination of alien architectural style and the climate and economic activities in China's southern towns, widely spread and developed in South China. It can be said that as long as the arcade-dwelling came into being, it bore, just like the watchtower, the obvious character of mixture of blood, a "symbiosis" of China's traditional culture and foreign culture.

Arcade house can be divided into 3 parts: pillar corridor, building body and housetop. The pillar corridor mixed the Chinese type and Western type. The decoration on some pillar heads is of the ancient Greek or Romanesque style. Other pillars are of round or square types of Chinese style. There were three methods to make the building body: the first was to open windows in the wall with a lot of Chinese or Western decorations; the second was to concave the building body to make outer corridor with a lot of ancient Greek or Romanesque style of pillars, as well as Islamic

The shopping street in Tangkou Town, Kaiping. The buildings were divided into three sections from upper part to the ground floor.

style; the third was to build the balcony. The shape of the balcony' plane and the bacony's railing style changed in thousand of ways, such as the style of square, the style of curve and so on. There are railing boards which bear the carving patterns, and there are

The pediment and the upmost wall of the arcade-house.

The tops of arcade-house with completely different style.

hollowed railing boards which are made of precast slabs, also there are iron-flower railings. The housetops of arcade-houses assume different shapes and postures. Most of them adopted simplified Western styles, even including the Western-style pavilions in microform.

Most of the arcade-houses are located in the commercial streets in the prosperous towns, so they were built on both sides of the streets. The high price of the land forced the building plane of arcade-house to develop towards the trends of "small front and deep, large inside". The airing, light, water supply and drainage would be dealt with within the house, mainly through courtyard, hall and corridors. This arrangement looked not good in terms of the high density of building, it is, however, quite suitable to the local climate. It is hot in summer in southern Guangdong Province, and the sun shines long during the day. The high wall and narrow lanes will have most area in the

The arcade-house with protruding balconies.

shadow of these buildings, and the deep and quiet courtyards have the fine air-raising effect, therefore the local residents could enjoy a bit coolness.

Walking among those arcade-houses, what people feel directly is the sense of entirety reflected by those zigzag arcade-dwellings. In other words, these houses offer fine visional sense of continuity. This mainly comes from the sense of prosody produced by the repetition of the small size of each house, i.e. the so-called effect of "row upon row". Though each shop front and the width of each front room are so different, yet the floors and height of the houses are nearly the same, the distance between shops is almost the same, thus giving a picture of prosperous commercial activities. This building group created by the local people really deserves the title of the "city design" of traditional society, marveled at by all contemporary architects.

In terms of the sightseeing of the towns, the "mix-up pattern" of different cultures reflected by the arcade-dwelling offers all kinds of things that appear so unrelated and even contradictive, forming a kind of life situation in dramatic style.

The arcade-house shopping street in Dihai Town which is winding and extending throughout the town.

The combination can be seen everywhere in the arcade-house shopping street in Chikan Town, Kaiping.

Different buildings mixed up, different shop signs come together, different shop owners shouted to sell their different goods, all of these seemed so untidy, while at the same time displayed some kind of vitality. It is the "mix" that brings the streets the interests of life and sense of humor. So far as the prosperity of the towns is concerned, such vigorous "mix" is beneficial and necessary.

Ancestral Temples Remain the Same Charisma

In the overseas Chinese hometown, the features of the mixture of the multi-cultures in the local buildings are not only reflected in the ordinary vernacular dwelling, but also in the traditional building of the ancestral temples – the local people's spiritual sustenance. The patriarchal system of thousands of years deep rooted in the heart of Chinese people. No matter who rose in position and fortune, he would seek for "returning to his hometown in glory", "fallen leaves that return to their roots", "returning to his hometown to hold a memorial ceremony for his ancestors" under the strong influence of patriarchal consciousness and the close blood relationship. This has been particularly stressed in those overseas Chinese. In those overseas Chinese, the influence of patriarchal consciousness is not negative totally, but has risen to the love of their kith and kin and the strong homesickness for their hometown, as well as the strong patriotic enthusiasm. In the early 20th century, countless overseas Chinese returned to their hometown to set up factories, open schools and engaged in public welfare, as a result, promoting the all-round development of the society, economy and culture of their hometown. Judged from the above facts, we can see that many overseas Chinese though physically were abroad, yet spiritually still at home. They succeeded to Chinese cultural tradition, once successful abroad, they would follow the tradition to build ancestral temples

The Charisma Hall in Kaiping.

at home or abroad to bring honor to their ancestors and encourage their descendants.

The peculiarities in the hometown of the overseas Chinese reflected its cultural and economic background. Those overseas Chinese lived abroad for a long time, having actively or passively accepted quite a little Western way of life and aesthetic judgment. The ancestral temples they built inevitably betrayed their ideological changes, as a result, there appeared "mixture of Oriental and Western elements" and "multi-combination" in the building's plane layout, decoration style, technique and material.

Among the extant ancestral temples built by the overseas Chinese and their relatives, the most stylish and famous one was the "Charisma Hall" in Kaiping, which was located in Jiaodizui Xu of Dihai Town, one of the three ports. It was a memorial building in memory of Yu family's ancestor – Yu Jing. According to the historical record, Yu Jing (A.D. 999-1064), a well-known minister in the Song Dynasty, born in Qujiang of Guangdong Province, also named An Dao, and named Wu Qi after death. In order to commemorate him, his descendants built a temple in Qujiang, named "Charisma Hall". From then on, Yu family's descendants at home and abroad all named memorial building "Charisma" or "Wu Qi" in memory of their ancestor. For example, in the United States, there is "Charisma Hall" and "Wu Qi Hall"; in Canada, there is "Yu Charisma Hall"; and in Guangzhou, there is "Wu Qi School".

The Charisma Hall was built by Chinese builders in the light of the Western style of buildings, a product of the cultural exchange of East and West through civilian channels. Owing to their less educated background, those traditional Chinese builders were less restrained by the so-called "regulations". Through combination of Eastern and Western building styles, the Hall appeared more lively and natural, novel and touching. The style and function of the Hall were the same as the traditional ones. The whole building was a large well-balanced "quadrangle", both independent and connected, with strict structure and magnificent grandness. The most

The details of decoration of the gate of the Charisma Hall.

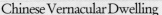
The rectangle-ear gables.

There are a lot of exquisite stone carvings on the base and banister of the entrance of the Charisma Hall.

important and successful feature of the building is its 18 well-designed fire-prevention walls. These fire-prevention walls originated from horse-head wall and absorbed the traditional *Fang'ershan* Wall of the local ancestral temples, hence resulted in the unique style.

In considering the building decorations, the different parts within the hall exposes the use of Chinese traditional crafts such as stone sculptures, wood sculptures, brick sculptures, pottery sculptures and iron castings, while detailed decoration reflected the Western building technique. For example, the top of the upmost part of the entrance to the lane is of Western pediment style and with scroll-type decorative sculptures; lower to it are small eaves of Chinese blazed tiles and Chinese-style wall pictures of mountains and water; still lower is the inscribed-board with Western decorations.

The pillars within the Hall were also masterpieces

風采堂

The *Xuan*, a combination of Chinese and Western cultural style in the Charisma Hall. The Western-style iron pillars support the Chinese glazed tile.

The coexistence of Chinese-style color painting and Western-style arch.

of the combination of Eastern and Western styles. Some pillar heads were decorated with flowers in classical Greek or Roman styles while the pillar bodies have no any sharp or mild concave troughs. At the same time some pillars were erected on typical Chinese pillar bases. The material of the pillars was mostly of stone. And there are a few iron pillars. For example, the half octagonal "*Xuan*" stretching out in front of the Hall is none other than the green blazed tile roof supported by four carved iron pillars, reflecting the use of new material and technology.

Making a comprehensive survey of the watchtower, arcade-dwelling and ancestral halls, one can see these buildings have one general character, that is, boldly absorbing the alien culture and merging it with local culture, so as to produce a new building culture. Most of the resident houses in Wuyi are "buildings without architects". Ordinary people were not restrained by "regulations" and trammels of conventional ideas, they made full use of whatever they thought useful. Although their efforts and practice were not surely to achieve desirable effects, yet this reflected their mentality of open-minded and the creativity of "seeking for something new, something changeable and something better".

by Yu Feng

The inner space and decoration details of the Charisma Hall.

5 Small Bridges, Flowing Streams and Cottages
– An Introduction to Shaoxing, an Area of Rivers and Lakes

◇ Three Thousand *Taimens* Originated from Shaoxing
◇ Small Bridges and Flowing Streams Accompany *Taimens*
◇ "Stage for All Ages" Close to Water at Shaoxing
◇ Looking after Ancient Heritages and Exploring Secluded Places

Shaoxing is a famous historical and cultural city in China, an area of rivers, lakes, bridges, yellow wines and local operas. It is rich in historical sedimentation and left a tremendous amount of human cultural heritages. As a material carrier of long historical culture, Shaoxing dwellings are embodiment of Shaoxing people's human essence of thousands of years, and reflect their particular philosophy of life and cause people's attention and thinking.

Shaoxing is situated at the northern foot of the Huiji Hill, and in the west of the Shaoning Plain on the southern bank of the Hangzhou Gulf in China. Shaoxing area has a dense population and is a traditional area of fish and rice. Shaoxing has a very long history and a great quantity of historical documents and records.

A specific geographical and historical conditions engendered a specific cultural circle and accelerated the formalization of folk houses at various places. Shaoxing is an important component of the cultural circle of the Han nationality in the south of the lower riches of the Changjiang River. The cultural and geographical position made Shaoxing dwellings belong to the system of non-beam-wood-framed construction. From the macro view, Shaoxing dwellings have some common features with their nearby folk dwellings, such as Huizhou dwellings and Suzhou dwellings. But from the micro view,

Shaoxing's geographical feature – a land where rivers densely distributed and the particular historical and cultural background gave its dwelling a strong specific character. It is just this condition that gestated such colorful Shaoxing which is like a life painting: small bridges, flowing streams and cottages.

The water land.

Three Thousand *Taimen*s Originated from Shaoxing

The local features of Shaoxing dwellings not only reflect in spatial form but also in their names. Generally, a larger house is called "*taimen*", but a simple and common cottage or humble room can not be called so. It is said that there were 3000 *taimen*s at old Shaoxing town, arranged in rows,

The river surface is as calm as mirror.

showing a prosperous scene of the southern region of
the lower riches of the Changjiang River. *Taimen*'s
plane distribution is as follows: along the principal axes
from the entrance to extend longitudinally, there are
gate, hall, main room and back hall in file; and at both
sides of the axes, there are usually bed rooms,
storerooms and kitchen. Patios, for interior aeration
and lighting in halls and rooms, links every row of
rooms. A larger *taimen* has five rows of rooms and
even much more. Combined with Chinese building's
traditional distribution – due north and south, Shaoxing
dwelling's plane is like a long and narrow rectangle
from north to south. For fireproof and guard against
theft, a *taimen*'s external walls are closed, especially
windows in gables are rarely opened; but the inner is
opened to patio, showing vitality.

The door-cover of *Taimen*.

The ways of traditional *taimen*'s naming varied and
approximately are four: in the light of official ranks; in
the light of trades, such as "sedan shop *taimen*", "tinfoil
paper *taimen*" and "pharmacy *taimen*"; in the light of
building's features, such as "bamboo-thread *taimen*",
"iron-plate *taimen*" and "the Eight Diagrams *taimen*";
in the light of surnames, such as *taimen* of family Wang,
taimen of family Zhang and *taimen* of family Lin, etc.
Because Chinese people always kept a tradition of all
members of a clan living together in a place, every
taimen had recorded the rise and fall of a family and
piled up innumerable historical stories. Up to day, many
*taimen*s are very incomplete and broken, their owners
are unknown, but the way and flavor of life filled in
those old *taimen*s were so simple and cordial, still
keeping the charm of ancient *Yue* culture.

The ancient taste still exists.

The majority of Shaoxing dwellings are one or two-
storied building, and the plane distribution is not strictly

Taimen of the Zhang family having witnessed many a historical changes.

symmetrical along the building's axes. When a man entered into the closed patio along the narrow and cool lane, he should feel enlightened suddenly. Not limited by general rule, designers adjusted measures to local conditions and treated with building distribution intelligently: patios being large or small, long or flat, make people find everything new and fresh when they enter by the stairs. Around the second floor of larger *taimen*'s patio, there was generally a connected cloister; all of these compose a special open system up and down, and the residents there can talk easily between two floors.

Among *taimen*s, there were usually narrow lanes, paved with blue flagstones. In the rainy season in April and May, lanes extended to far in continuous drizzle, which is very like a Chinese painting of misty rain. The lower part of gables at both sides of lanes, namely the dado of the external walls was made of stone for protecting the inner brick wall.

The exquisite *taimen*s have more wood-carvings and stone carvings, which are an important manifestation of folk artisan's techniques. The woodcarving was principally used in building's accessorial components, such as door and window partition board or batter brace, with themes of lucky designs, animals and historical personalities and so on, which skill very fine and images lifelike. The majority of woodcarvings were not painted. Some of them kept the original color of wood and had turned into dark brown step by step after long time; others, such as partition boards, painted by black paint showed a charm of primitive simplicity foiled by white walls. Stone carving was usually used on doorcover and ridge, generally as decorative components. Many folk houses have stone-carved lattice windows, which designs were basically linear veins, serving as a foil to

The deep narrow Lane.

Woodcarving on architectural components.

their central characters or mascots, very symmetrical and fine.

Some scholars point out that Shaoxing's architectural art is an art of "black, white and gray colors". In truth, when the people walk on traditional settlements of dwellings, they see white walls, black tiles, darkgray stone-bridges, dark brown partition-boards and "the culture of three black things" proper in Shaoxing (black-awninged boats on the rivers, black hat on the people's head and black dried vegetable sending forth aroma in many houses) and feel a silent and elegant flavor of the south of the lower reaches of the Changjiang River. "The culture of three black things" and black, white and gray colors exerted a subtle influence on local aesthetic conception, which gradually turned implicative, wide,

The exquisite stone carving.

The black-awninged boat.

thick and profound; the residents' heart seems purified much, far from flippancy, not seeking fame and wealth but keeping their ideals. In full-bodied ambient of a land of rivers and lakes, fellow townsmen row boats drinking yellow wines, looking so low-pressured. It seems that any bagatelle in life has been cast to the winds.

The Old Shaoxing people.

Small Bridges and Flowing Streams Accompany *Taimen*s

The greatest feature of Shaoxing dwelling is that folk houses are closely linked with rivers and bridges. More exactly saying, these three factors are close symbiosis.

River network covers Shaoxing area densely and for this reason Shaoxing has a very famous name – "a land rich in riverlets". Today, in Shaoxing area there are the Cao'e River, the Puyang River and the Jian Lake, all of which inflow into the Qiantang

Small bridge, flowing stream and households.

River; the East Zhejiang Channel crosses the north of Shaoxing area from the east to the west and communicates with the rivers flowing from the north to the south, forming a river system with high density of rivers in the northern plain of Shaoxing area. Consistently, Shaoxing has been very famous for her natural beauty of lakes and hills, as some verses describe: "The hills at Shaoxing are green and rivers clear for ever".

With developed water conservancy facilities and good irrigation works, today's Shaoxing is called a land of swamps but she does not suffer from inundation nor waterlog. When the people selected the position for living together, the first thing that they thought was to be close to water and many folk houses face to a river, or are backed by a river or even span a river. According to statistics, over 80% of 2500 natural villages are close to rivers or ponds. In Shaoxing, river streets, river lanes, river villages can be found everywhere. For Shaoxing people, rivers are important productive factor as well as communications net and organic component of housing conditions.

Shaoxing traditional dwellings were generally built along rivers. According to the relations between land and water communication systems, there are three cases: "a river with two streets", "a river with one street" and "a river without any street". In towns with dense population, the total depth of a *taimen* was generally equal to the width of the building block close to the river. The architectural layout of a *taimen* is as follows: the front door faces to street and the back door to the river. The front side of the house was used as a shop and the back side close to the river

A river with two streets.   A river with one street.

was for stocking goods through rivers. Traditional streets are narrow, suitable to walking; and the rivers to the backside of *taimen*s were for sailing boats, like today's motorways. Seeing the highly efficient communication system of "men walk and boats navigate respectively along their own way" of old times, we have to wonder the ability and wisdom of ancient *Yue* people.

In the planning structure of traditional dwellings of "a river with two streets" and "a river with one street", the streets were between folk houses and rivers, playing a role of land communications and serving as the entrance and exit of water transportation. The later function was realized by river wharves. There are a large number of river wharves at Shaoxing, very helpful to residents to use water in life and go on board. At some sections, every 4-5 meters there is a river-wharf averagely, how high is the density! At some prosperous sections in the past times, such as Keqiao and Anchang at Shaoxing, some long corridors with windows were set up for keeping out wind and rain. Looking at them from afar, the long corridors with dark color extend to the far, uniting the houses close to rivers.

In traditional quarter of dwellings, rivers were inseparable with bridges. Shaoxing has a great number of bridges distributed over wide areas. The Map of Streets at Shaoxing Prefecture Town drawn in 1892 shows that there were 229 bridges at Shaoxing Town, every five steps there was a stone-bridge and every ten steps, an arch-bridge. It is said that: "There is not a town without bridge, not a road without bridge and not a village without bridge". Now, Shaoxing is one of the areas which have kept the most kinds and quantity of ancient bridges, including wood-beam bridges, wood-arch bridges, stone-beam bridges,

The long corridor.

The bridge in the shape of Chinese character " 八 " in Shaoxing.

The Map of Streets at Shaoxing Prefecture Town.

polygonal bridges, semi-round stone-arch bridges, U-shaped bridges and elliptoid stone-arch bridges, etc. which constitute a complete system of ancient bridges. So Shaoxing is called a "museum of Chinese ancient bridges".

77

In distribution, Shaoxing's bridges and buildings compose an organic entirety. For example, a bridge like Chinese character "八" (eight), located at the east of Shaoxing Town and built in the Song Dynasty, is the earliest urban bridge existing now in China: both sides of the bridge inclines face to face, like a Chinese character " 八 ", so called *Bazi* (eight) Bridge. The whole bridge spans three rivers and links three streets, being a real crossroads in ancient times. It is a rare design, because the designer solved the problem of communication better on the one hand, and did not occupied many land used for building houses on the other hand. The other example is a small stone bridge at Anchang; an approach bridge at one side of this bridge extends into two folk houses on the bank; viewing from the opposite bank, the form and colors of the houses are very harmonious, the houses are like bridge towers, merging into one organic whole with the bridge.

The Anchang ancient bridge.

"Stage for All Ages" Close to Water at Shaoxing

Shaoxing is a very famous land of local operas, such as traditional Xinchang Opera, Shaoxing Play with an out-and-out charm and Shaoxing Opera, the second most important local opera in China. The prosperity of local operas at Shaoxing promoted the construction of many stages. The famous writer Lu Xun (1881-1936) described vividly in his work *Village Theatrical*

78

Performance: "The most attractive thing is a stage standing at an area close to a river outside the village, which is standing faintly in the distance in the moon night, and can hardly be seprated from the surrounding. I doubt that the wonderland which I saw in pictures emerges there". At Shaoxing area,

Stage and village theatrical performance.

ancient stages have a particular name – "stage for all ages", which symbolizes local operas' unceasing continuity and eternal development.

Shaoxing's "stage for all ages" was generally set up on the axis of a certain series of buildings, facing to a temple or a clan ancestral hall, an enclosed ground was used for spectators to see operas. The stage consists of two parts: the foreside is an open high platform, from which spectators of three sides can see the performance on the stage; and the backside is closed rooms – rest-room, dressing room, property room and in addition serves as stage's background. The frontage of a stage must be toward a temple and the back must facilitate the opera troupe to convey dressing and property boxes easily from boats on rivers. Many stages have carved beams and painted rafters, very delicate and refined.

Shaoxing's ancient stages included stages close to rivers, stages in clan ancestral halls and stages in temples. Among them, the ones most close to common people's life and best reflected the features of a land of rivers and lakes were stages close to rivers distributed at towns. Their location was usually near a bridge or at a small square close to a bridgehead. This location could economize investment and easily evacuate spectators and at the same time, the high bridge itself is a best stand. Shaoxing's ancient stages are an inseparable part of the whole environment of traditional housing estate, providing the Shaoxing people a basic place for rest and entertainment, and propagated the people feudal morality and ethics by sermons in local operas. As a local culture, they were a way to express local people's ideals and desires. Their architectural form exhibited fully the agile, unpredictable and delicate

The stage by the river.

features of buildings at the land of rivers and lakes. Their combination with rivers in different positions formed an organic part of the whole prospect of a land of rivers and lakes.

According to the relationship among stage, the environment of construction site, rivers and roads, the stages close to river can be classified in four kinds: stage with three sides close to river; stage spanning the river; stage spanning a street; and stage set up at the center of a river. A stage with three sides close to river is most popular, such as *Ancheng* Stage at Mashan District of Shaoxing County. If the ground for spectators was narrow, the platform would be set up in the river, where three sides close to river and a side near the riverbank. The facade of a stage usually faces to the riverbank, but some stages were located with their sides toward riverbank, some even with the back to the riverbank. Why must a stage adopt this form? The reason is that most public places at Shaoxing's traditional settlements are lineal streets and squares can hardly be found; but a large ground is necessary for local operas' performance, so a stage set up in the river could accept more spectators.

In a place where the land for construction is insufficient and close to a narrow river, the stage was usually set up directly across the river, such as the *Longjinzhuang* Stage on the Nanshan hilltop near the southern gate of Shaoxing Town. The local operas were acted on this stage. When boats were sailing through the stage, a poetic scenery of a land of rivers and lakes came into view. A stage spanning a street was the most interesting one: at ordinary times, it served as a street pavilion, and when it's time to act local operas, the stage board would be added. The example is the *Tuguci* Stage, very well reserved up to day. The stages set up in the center of river were casually installed for some particular occasions, for example the stage in a river written by Mr. Lu Xun in his work *Village Theatrical Performance*.

Looking after Ancient Heritages and Exploring Secluded Places

Shaoxing is very known as "a land of fish and rice", but even more known as "an remarkable place producing outstanding people" and "a place where celebrities gather together" in China. The culture of a long history created by celebrities left a lot of former residences of celebrities, such as the Mansion of Lü, the *Qingteng* Study, the former residence of Lu Xun, the *Sanwei* Study, the former residence of Wang Xizhi (321-379), a very famous calligrapher in ancient China, and so on. Among them, some are folk houses or mansions with impressive appearance; some are scholar's studies with aroma of Chinese ink; and others are houses close to river with Shaoxing's traditional charm. These former residences of celebrities spread all over the land of the Shaoxing region like stars in the sky, telling the people the brilliant past of Shaoxing and demonstrating its fine future.

The famous Mansion of Lü at Shaoxing, a residence of Lü Ben, a minister in the Jiajing reign of the Ming Dynasty (1522-1566), is a typical representative of vernacular mansions. On the east, the mansion of Lü started from the *Wan'an* Bridge to the *Xiegong* Bridge on the west, on the south starting from Xinhe Lane to the Dayou Storehouse on the north. There were two channels of water and a street in the mansion area. The whole mansion is composed of 13 halls and rooms in rows, called "Thirteen Halls of

The former residence of Xu Xilin immerged in green plants.

Mansion Lü". From the entrance's stairs to enter, along the central axis from the south to north, there were Sedan Hall, *Yong'en* Hall, the Third Hall, the Fourth Hall and the Fifth Hall in turn; and there are five buildings along left and right axes respectively. Its patios were large, halls commodious, materials solid, reflecting some features of official mansions in the southern China in the Ming Dynasty. In addition, because this mansion was located at a land of rivers and lakes, it merged some fresh, lucid, lively, elegant and simple features of Shaoxing dwellings.

The *Qingteng* Study is a typical representative of garden-style folk dwellings, with a superficies of less than two *mu*, a silent, elegant and uncommon environment, full of strong human flavor. This study was the birth and study place of Xu Wei (1521-1593), a famous calligrapher, painter and litterateur in the Ming Dynasty. Besides, Chen Hongshou (1598-1652), a great painter in the late Ming Dynasty and the early Qing Dynasty, also lived here for admiring its reputation. The study was an one-storied house built against the hill, with stonecolumns, brickwalls and wood grilles; it had two rooms: the fore room facing south, a figure of Xu Wei, a script written by him "Not Soiled by a Speck of Dust" and a horizontal inscribed-board written by Chen Hongshou were hanging on the wall. There is a called "Heaven Pool" in the patio outside of the southern windows, Xu Wei said: "the pool has no bottom, not dry even in arid days, some divinities seem in it". The well, the bench,

the door, the pool, and the vine, are with simple form but comprehensive meanings, show fully the extraordinary artistic savor and garden technique of this painting master.

The former residence of Lu Xun, *Sanwei* Study, *Baicao* Garden and the ancestral house of Lu Xun are the birth and growth place of Mr. Lu Xun, an eminent writer of China. They showed

A well, a bench, a gate, a pond and a vine.

the true aspect of common folk houses at Shaoxing in Lu Xun's adolescent times. Many times, Lu Xun described these places in his works, such as the very known essay *From Baicao Garden to Sanwei Study.* The *Sanwei* Study was a famous private school at Shaoxing in the late Qing Dynasty, where Lu Xun studied from 12-17 years old. The former residence of Lu Xun and *Sanwei* Study were houses with white walls, black tiles, and columns painted with black paint, simple and elegant, reflecting sufficiently Shaoxing traditional dwelling's dimensional form in the late Qing Dynasty and the early years of the Republic of China. The *Baicao* Garden is located at the back of the former residence of Lu Xun, originally a

The front gate of Sanwei Study.

vegetable garden where young Lu Xun played frequently, tasting amaranthine mulberry and sweet but vinegary raspberry, capturing crickets and pulling out poligonum multiflorum. These interesting things in childhood left nice and indelible impressions in Lu Xun's mind and make people taste the life in old traditional dwellings from children's visual angle.

Shaoxing dwellings are situated at the residential environment full of poetic and artistic conception, built by ancestors of the ancient *Yue* region on the base of their deep understanding of the environment of land of rivers and lakes; furthermore they are a group of vivid life scenes and a high-grade culture continued for long times.

by Yu Feng

6 Imposing Dwellings and Spacious Courtyard

– A Visit of the Residential Quadrangle

◇ The Imposing Dwellings and Spacious Courtyards
◇ Knock at the Door Leaves
◇ Floral-Pendant Gate Letting People's Mind at Ease
◇ A Place of Unique Beauty

From the commencement of large-scale city construction after the Yuan Dynasty formally made Beijing its capital, the residential quadrangle emerged with the palaces, government office buildings, street blocks and lanes in Beijing. According to the decrees of Kublai Khan, the founder of the Yuan Dynasty, the residents who moved to the old Beijing were rich men or high-ranking officials who had the priority to get 8.1 *mu* land, where they could build the private residential. The traditional residential quadrangles rose in Beijing.

Aside from the Forbidden City, Imperial Gardens, Monastery, Temples, Dwellings of royal family and government office buildings, the numerous buildings in old Beijing were the residential houses of the common people which take the form of quadrangles. Since the Ming and Qing dynasties, though the quadrangles in Beijing had experienced many vicissitudes of life, the basic living styles were already formulated; having undergone continuous improvement the unique vernacular dwelling was presented before us.

The mode of quadrangle was characterized by its solemnness, elegance, reasonable arrangement, as well as peaceful and secluded environment. The ancient romantic charm of the quadrangle in Beijing was contained in its high steps, gate stone, scarlet arch, blue bricks, grey tiles, bargeboard (*An often ornamented board that conceals roof timber projecting over gables.*), high-rising ridge ornaments like horsetails, landscape paintings under the

The main entrance of the quadrangle.

Groups of quadrangles.

eaves, rubbed brickwork, and ingenious and delicate gardens...

The Imposing Dwellings and Spacious Courtyards

The quadrangles in Beijing had their internal links with grid arrangement of chessboard-shaped streets. A normal quadrangle was facing the south in line with land heading from the east to the west.

With symmetrical central axis, balanced left and right sides the quadrangle is closed to the outside, internally centripetal and square-shaped. The scale of the quadrangles varied from each other while their sizes registered large difference, but no matter that they were big or small, all of them were composed of basic units.

A courtyard surrounded by houses was the basic unit of residential quadrangle, which was called "*Yi Jin Si*

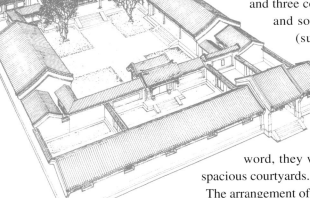

A bird's-eye view of the middle-sized quadrangle.

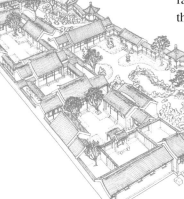

A bird's-eye view of the large-sized quadrangle with a garden.

He Yuan" (the residential quadrangle with one courtyard); while the quadrangle composed of two courtyards were regarded as *Er Jin Si He Yuan*, and three courtyards, *San Jin Si He Yuan* and so forth. The large quadrangle (such as Residence of a royal family) might have seven to nine courtyards. Aside from the main yard situated at the center, there were side yards in the east and west sides; in a word, they were imposing dwellings and spacious courtyards.

The arrangement of the quadrangle in Beijing was relatively fixed. Generally speaking, the quadrangle consists of the principal rooms, the aisles, the wingrooms, the back cabinet house, and the inverted rooms.

Due to the influence of the sunshine, the houses facing the sun in a quadrangle are the best, therefore the northern rooms were usually chosen as the principal rooms while the wing rooms were situated on the east and west sides of the quadrangle. The principal rooms were most important dwellings. Because the memorial tablets of the ancestor and the hall were in the central part of the principal rooms, the principle rooms occupied the highest position in the whole residence. The space, depth and height of the principal rooms were larger or longer than other rooms. The principal rooms were composed of three rooms, in the central was the hall

A view of the principal rooms, the east and west wing rooms and the courtyard from the floral-pendant gate.

storing the memorial tablets of their ancestors, and on the eastern side stood the living room of grandparents, wile on its west wing situated the living room of father and mother. The room on the left side were larger than the one on the right. This was resulting from the traditional conception of the left being more superior. In the quadrangle, aside from the hall on the central axis, the eastern house was regarded as the secondly good rooms.

The rooms situated in front of the principal rooms, and expanded the space of yard were called wing rooms. Wing rooms was usually composed of three rooms where the younger generations lived.

At two sides of the principal rooms usually stood the aisles. Just like the principal rooms, the aisles were usually facing the south. The only difference is their spaces are smaller. In other words, their back walls are parallel to the principal rooms while their front walls were shrunk from the principal rooms. Because they are narrow in depth, the height of them is lower too. If the principal rooms were likened to a human face, then, the aisles were two ears of human being. There may stand one aisle on each side of the principal rooms, which was called "three rooms in the open and five rooms in secret". In other words, at initial glance, we can see three rooms, but as a matter

The aisle, the small patio and the veranda.

of fact, the principal rooms were composed of 5 rooms. Of course, there may also stand two aisles on each side of the principal rooms, which was called "three rooms in the open and 7 rooms in secret". Just in front of the aisles was the northern gable of the eastern wing rooms or west wing rooms. The east and west sides of the small space between the aisles and the gables of wing rooms were separated by courtyard walls and the verandas, which formed a small yard before the aisles. The unpaved ground in the yard was called "open-air ground", where flowers and trees were planted by the landlords. In the meantime the aisles were the studies of a number of scholars because they had a very good reading environment with direct sunshine and a small space that could keep good secret.

The aisles were usually linked to the secondary rooms of the principal rooms. The principal rooms and aisles had independent gables. But, after the founding of the Republic of China in 1911, the structure of the quadrangle inclined to simplification, for instance, two gables had combined into one.

The principal rooms and wing rooms were linked by the fold-arm veranda, which was an attached open structure that might be the corridor, or a place where people may have a rest or appreciate the delightful scenery.

The house at the back of the principal rooms was called "back cabinet house", which were composed of many rooms. The back cabinet house located at the back place of courtyard were mainly living rooms for girls or maidservants, the back cabinet house could keep secrets very well. The girls were placed under rigid supervision of their parents because they should pass through the principal rooms where their parents lived if they desired to go out. The back cabinet house was secondly to the wing rooms in terms of its grade, therefore, it was smaller than the wing rooms. If the back of a quadrangle was facing the street, a house on the northwest corner could serve as the backdoor. The wall of the quadrangle adjacent to the street usually had no window at all, sometimes only had high small windows; the passer-by could not see anything inside of the rooms.

The back cabinet house were situated in the north end of the courtyard while the opposite rooms in the southern end were called "inverted rooms". Those inverted rooms were arranged in the following order: the room on the east end was given to private school; the second room counting from the east was the gate; the room just in the opposite of the *chui hua men*(floral-pendant gate) was the living room of man servant; the rooms next to man servant room and in the opposite of three principal

88

rooms were guest rooms, which sometimes were used as reception rooms. The room at the west end of the inverted rooms was the toilet separated by wall running from the South to North. It had a small gate, which was called Moon Gate. In superstition, the southwest corner was the place of five ghosts' abode. The filthiness of the toilet could suppress the disturbances created by the right white tiger (according to the ancient Chinese myths, there were four spirits who guarded at the four directions: the green dragon on the left; white tiger on the right, rose finch in the front and tortoise in the back.).

The quadrangle with more than two courtyards could be divided into internal residence and external residence, while they were connected by two gates: floral-pedant gate and screen gate.

The golden-column gate.

Knock at the Door Leaves

If you were walking in a lane of old Beijing you might find the closed door leaves on the way. Such an atmosphere and feelings of tranquility was typical of Beijing flavor.

From time to time Chinese people paid special attention to gate, which was the face of the vernacular dwelling and symbolization of the social status. The social status of a household head could be distinguished from the style, size, roof shapes, color of paints and ornaments of the gate.

According to scale and rank the quadrangle gates could be divided into *wangfu* (royal family) gate, brilliant gate, golden-column gate and *ruyi* gate ("s" shaped ornamental gate). The *wangfu* gate, brilliant gate and golden-column gate were most possessed by the kings, princes and aristocrats and bureaucratic

The *Ruyi* gate.

strata, while the *ruyi* gate was erected by businessmen or rich merchants. The gate of the quadrangle was just like a small house that could be called house-shaped gate.

Brilliant gate was the highest ranking gate second only to *wangfu* gate, while it could only be built in front of residence of certain ranking officials in the Qing Dynasty. Generally speaking, the gate of the quadrangle in Beijing was one of the inverted rooms. This room was deeper than the rooms next to it and with a higher roof; while the walls at two sides of the gate protruding as ornament. Something was put under the ground of the gate to raise its level, which was higher than the street or lane outside the gate. If you come out of the quadrangle

The drum stone.

you may have a feeling of occupying a commanding position; if you enter the quadrangle, you may have a sense of ascending a height. The part near the lower part of the roofing and on the front of the gables located at the two sides of the gate caved in a little , which was called "*Chitou* (step)". The *Chitou* was usually ornamented with brick carving. The contents of the brick carving fell into two categories: praying for happiness, or avoiding evil spirits.

The special feature of the brilliant gate was that the gate stood between the gable columns under the ridge purlin. The gate opening was divided into two: half outside of the gate and half inside of the gate. The lower end of gate axis was placed on the pit of gate pillow stone while the upper end was bound with needle beam (*Needle beam was kind of ornament decorated on the gate of the quadrangle or some small courtyards.*) and

The petty lion on the gate pillow stone.

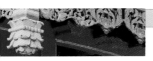
90

principal column. Four different shaped needle beams decorated with wood carvings were widely used. A pair of drum stone (*Drum stone is a kind of gate pillow stone, whose upper part was shaped like a drum.*) stood outside of door leaves. The drum stone was the ornament at both sides of the gate. The needle beams coupled well with the drum stone and added endless charm to the gate.

Most brilliant gate had no ceilings while people can look up at the structure under the roof. A half-suspended ceiling might be fixed. The suspended ceiling was usually fixed under the roof inside of the gate, therefore it was designated as half-suspended ceiling. The roof of the gate of the quadrangle in Beijing was *Yingshan*

The screen wall.

roof (*Yingshan roof was a kind of Chinese roof characterized by not protruding outside the gable.*) using cylindrical tiles. The steps were outside of the gate while the flag stones with vertical stripes and slopes were paved at the two sides of the steps.

The golden-column gate was more ingenious than the brilliant gate. The most outer column of the building was the peripheral column, the column supporting the roof ridge in the center was called newel while the golden column standing between the peripheral column and the newel. The gate with gate leaves fixed on the golden column was called the golden-column gate. In both directions of the newel always stood the golden column. The golden column gate in the quadrangle in Beijing was fixed on the outer golden column between the newel and outer peripheral column. Such a gate was characterized by shallow passageway out of the gate leaves and deep passageway behind the gate leaves. Other ornaments of the golden column gate was similar to those of the brilliant gate, except that a suspended ceiling was installed. Especially on the padding board among the suspended ceiling, eaves purlins and *efang* out of the gate leaves was painted with colorful picture in Suzhou style.

The screen wall was a brick-structured wall with strong ornamental and symbolizing significance in front

The exquisite floral-pendant gate.

of the gate of the quadrangle in Beijing. Its main function was to beautify the entrance of the gate, people might see the carved auspicious words or eulogies or decorated ornaments on the wall face.

The screen wall served as contrast to the gate while the latter would serve as contrast to the former, they could not be separated from each other. The screen wall was only a wall, but it played a role of foiling the quadrangle because of its ingenious and delicate structure.

Floral-Pendant Gate Letting People's Mind at Ease

The floral-pendant gate was an elegant gate of the quadrangle in Beijing being characterized by its dignity and beauty, which served as the demarcation of outer courtyard and the inner residence.

The floral-pendant gate was built on the main axis of the quadrangle while it was situated at the middle north side of the outer courtyard, and laid on the three strata or five strata steps of greenish marble serving as the demarcation of the front court and inner court.

The front court was the place for guest reception while the inner court was the living quarters for family members, where the strangers were not allowed to enter, even the servants, had no exception. The old saying goes that "the servants could not got out of the gate and enter into the second gate". The second gate referred to the floral-pendant gate.

Two functions were played by the floral-pendant gate. One was the defending function. Between two columns on the exterior side fixed the first successive gate which was very thick, just like the street gate, while it was called "chessboard gate" or "polygonal gate", which was opened to communications in the daytime and was closed at night for safety.

Secondly it played the role of screening, which was the main function of the floral-pendant gate. In

The Lotus-pendent Column (l).

92

The Lotus-pendent Column (II).

order to guarantee the privacy, between the two columns on the interior side fixed the second successive gate called "the screening gate". Except for the magnificent rites like wedding and funerals that needed to open it, the screening gate was closed all the time, when people entered or came out the second gate they usually passed the side doors beside the screening gate or passed through the veranda beside the screening gate to the inner court and rooms. This function of the floral-pendant gate was played to fully link the outer residences while having rigidly divided the space.

Viewing from its shape it was called "floral-pendant gate" because the peripheral column was suspended, while it was embellished with beautiful wood carvings such as lotus petals and lotus leaves.

In the meantime, the floral-pendant gate was a building for ornamentation, as all its projecting parts were embellished with the delicate ornaments. The exterior side of beam head was carved in a shape of rosy clouds that was named as "hemp-leaf beam head" and was rarely seen in other kind of buildings. Under the hemp-leaf beam head there was a pair of short overhanging columns with a downward pillar head carved with lotus petals, strings of pearls and floriation, just like the flower bud to open. This pair of short columns was called "lotus-pendant column". The name of the floral-pendant gate perhaps was derived from the specific pendant columns.

The floral-pendant gate was located at the central axis of the whole courtyard. It is splendid and conspicuous and could be the embodiment of the finance and cultural cultivation as well as the hobby and character

The profound courtyard with an elegant tast.

of the residential owner.

Through the small floral-pendant gate we can see the industrious, wise and intelligent Chinese people of ancient times, and a series of picture scrolls of folk custom with strong national flavor.

A Place of Unique Beauty

A plot of land was enclosed by the dwellings, winding corridors and surrounding walls forming a unified space – the quadrangle.

The frost-free period in Beijing lasted about 200 days and all the year round it is suitable for the outdoor activities. And moreover, because of long sunshine time, the courtyard dwellings were more suitable to live in. Because of bitter cold and slant sunlight in winter the courtyard was quite wide and spacious so that all the buildings could receive more sunshine with less shelter.

The sunlight shining into the room not only could increase the temperature of the room, but also make people in the room feel warm-hearted

The former dwelling of a famous scholar covered by green leaves.

spiritually. The quadrangle in Beijing was secluded from the outside with windows open to the courtyard. This is an effective measure against the sand storm. The courtyard is the core of the family life. Therefore, the construction of the courtyard showed special esthetic taste.

Attention was paid to planting flowers and trees in the courtyard to form a good environment sheltered by trees and flowers. The four square plots of land at the four corners of the courtyard were reserved for planting without any stone pavement. The most favorite flowers of the old Beijing Men included lilac, Chinese flowering crabapple, flowering plum, mountain peach flower, while the most favorite trees of

old Beijing Men included jujube tree, Chinese scholar tree and cherry apple tree, among them the cherry apple tree was regarded the most orthodox which was the symbol of harmony between brothers. Up to the modern times more kinds of trees were planted in Beijing. All flowering plants and trees with fruits were welcomed by the people in Beijing.

Miniature trees and rocky was the special trait of the quadrangle in Beijing. A saying of the Qing Dynasty goes that "canopy, fish jar, pomegranate tree, lords, fat dogs and fat girls" which is the vivid picture of the quadrangle in Beijing. The fish jar not only bred golden fishes but also planted lotus. The potted flowers and trees included pomegranate trees, rosebay orange osmanthus, bay tree, azalea, cape jasmine , and so on. The pomegranate trees were planted in big flower pots covered with green-painted wood bucket. Pomegranate tree lovers mainly prayed for more children because of the numerousness of seeds in pomegranate fruit. In the winter, all these flowers and trees would move into houses.

The cosy indoor space.

The four-o'clock, morning glory, hyacinth bean flower in front of steps were the common pretty scenery of the quadrangle in Beijing.

The ideal traditional living style of the Chinese people was the quadrangle composed of houses, courtyard, first gate, second gate, verandas, private school, drawing room, screen wall, warehouse, kitchen, even gardens or stabes in big families. The quadrangle was a closed residence with a gate toward the street. If the gate was closed, the quadrangle would be a small world that could keep good secret and was ideal to the inhabitation of the whole family.

by Zhao Zhifeng

7 Natural Rhythm and Intelligent Conversion
— Inspections on *Zhang* Dwelling in Central Yunnan

◇ Abode Groveling on the Mother Earth
◇ Homestead Where Souls Reposed
◇ The Conversion to Nature

There are lots of beautiful places, such as Dali, Li Jiang, Xishuangbanna, etc., which enchant tourists. But when you visit Central and South Yunnan areas and go deep into the Ailao Mountain, the Red River's drainage areas, the scenery composed of alps, flowing water, terraced fields and houses will attract you, and you will find that here is also so fine. There are good mountains, good waters, and good folkways here. This portion of beauty contains boldness, sturdiness and grittiness, which make you generate deep affection.

The cloud sea, the terraced fields and the ancient *Butou* road of world wonder can be found here. Even the distinct charm of *Tu Zhang* Dwelling villages, which dispersivedly locate in canyons and seem growing out from mountain soil, can be appreciated.

Abode Groveling on the Mother Earth

The Ailao Mountain ranges are rising and falling, while the sceneries across the Red River straits are grand and rare. The weather is genial, rainfall is abundant, and forest is exuberant here. Since thousands of years, people of different nationalities, such as Yi, Hani, Dai, Miao, Yao, Zhuang and Han, etc. have lived in these high mountain ridges for generations. And the *Tu Zhang* Dwellings are their abodes and

The mushroom houses of the Hani nationality.

homesteads, which are built among the natural environment.

Generally speaking, compared with residences with exquisite forms in some regions of Yunnan (such as Bai nationality's dwellings in Dali area, western Yunnan), the *Tu Zhang* Dwelling obviously is simple and economical. Even compared with riverside-courtyard dwelling at almost the same area, the *Tu Zhang* Dwelling is much more inferior in terms of refinement. However, the *Tu Zhang* Dwelling's satisfaction toward living logic, adaptation toward productivity condition, and relation with the surrounding environment naturally show Yi and Hani people's sincerity

The settlement in the Ailao Mountains of the Red River basin.

The *Tuzhang*-Dwelling village following the topography of the mountain.

toward living, and have even reflected their intelligence in creating and harnessing their own lives.

This is a kind of flat-roof house with soil-wood structure, commonly called *Tu Zhang* Dwelling because its roof is spread with rammed soil. Typical feature of *Tu Zhang* Dwelling is the rectangle plane surface composed of main house and wing-house. The main house consists of three open rooms and is mostly two-storied structure. The wing-house generally is single-storied one. The room structure mostly is wood framework, but wall bodies are mostly brick walls on soil-base, or rammed clay walls. Pillars inside the room are wood. Some wood girders are laid on the roof, cleft timbers are put between girders, green pine hairs are spread and clay mixed with grass and soil cover the wood girders and are rammed by hammers. The flat-roof is flat and neat, stout and solid with perfect waterproof function. The *Tu Zhang* Dwelling's building materials are indigenous, such as local soils and timbers. The *Tu Zhang Dwelling*'s structure and building techniques are simple, the cost of its construction is low, the building technique is in line with local conditions while being easy to grasp. Nearly 80-90% of minorities' dwellings at the Ailao Mountains are *Tu Zhang* Dwellings.

Soils and timbers the *Tu Zhang* Dwelling used are very convenient for local people, which can be renewed at any moment and can regress to nature. All of these materials have tenacity, which not only can be made into natural shielding materials, but also are easy to be processed and

The *Tu Zhang* Dwellings are in perfect harmony with the environment naturally.

98

use. Immature soils and timbers are gifts of nature, and it conforms to natural logic to utilize the gifts to build shields. There are lots of dwellings and villages built of soils in North-west China and Tibet, Middle-east and ancient Babylon regions. All of these houses

The entrance of the *Tu Zhang* Dwelling.

built of soil materials are called "immature soils building" by architects and the *Tu Zhang* Dwelling is one typical "immature soils building".

Inside the *Tu Zhang* Dwelling, wood pillars and wood girders form the structure system, whose arrangement relates to space required by life. For instance, the *Tu Zhang* Dwellings with a two-storied structure are commonly found, the first floor for bedroom, living room and kitchen, the second floor for depository and sundries. Whether soil house or

The principal room and aisle of the *Tu Zhang* Dwelling.

grass house, the middle room among three big open rooms must be central room, which is used for receiving guests, dining or feting, and the right and the left ones are bedroom and kitchen. There are other rooms for cattle, horse, pig and chicken. Yi and Hani People not only let wood structure serve as force-bearing structure, but also let it serve the actual requirement for dwelling and sheltering. So, when building a new house, the Yi people will certainly choose a lucky day: vertical pillar and girder are set up at night, roof truss is set up before dawn, and top girder is raised in next day's morning. During raising top girder, a piece of deep red cloth is enlaced in the middle of the top girder. The girder is raised to the peak of house in firecrackers' sound.

Most of *Tu Zhang* Dwellings spread over the mountainsides of big mountains. Because there is not a vast expanse of plains, and there are layers upon layers of terraces, lands for villages are very limited. So, the flat-roof of *Tu Zhang* Dwelling becomes another kind of location for domestic work. This platform can not only air and bask crops, but also carry out many family activities. On the platform, there are not only many crops such as paddy, corn, buckwheat, miscellaneous bean, vegetable, melon and fruits, but

The interesting walking system in the air.

A continous platform formed by the roofs of *Tu Zhang* Dwellings.

also people working busily or taking a rest with families, which exhibit an agreeable atmosphere and vision of family life. What is more miraculous is that most of the flatroofs in villages are connected by wood ladders. Thus, an "air transportation system" is formed. Therefore, guests often descend from

Many a family activities are performed on the roof of *Tu zhang* Dwelling.

air. We cannot help but gasp in admiring villagers' imagination and creativity during house building.

Because of right selection of materials, structure and constructing mode, the *Tu Zhang* Dwelling's wall and house face have good heat-storage ability, adapting to local xerothermic river valley climate. It doesn't become hot under solarization, doesn't let cold wind in, and can not be drenched by rain. The *Tu Zhang* Dwelling is warm in winter and cool in summer. All of these

The wall of the *Tu zhang* Dwelling.

A overlook of the *Tu Zhang* Dwelling village.

are highly fit for dwelling and daily living for human being. The local people vividly say that the *Tu Zhang* Dwelling seems as a heat preservation kettle.

The *Tu Zhang* Dwelling has soil wall and roof, and is solid and massy, the wall has no window or just small window. Viewing from far away, there is a stretch of reddish yellow, which appears profound and rustic, and has a kind of inherent and stout appeal and aesthetic feeling.

Homestead Where Souls Reposed

For people in *Tu Zhang* Dwelling villages, these architectures are not only their lives' abode, but also their spiritual homestead.

Many scholars think that the *Tu Zhang* Dwelling and co-generic mushroom house in Red River valley of Yunnan should be a kind of variant of ancient cave abode, which is reconstructed by Yi and Hani nationalities who are descendants of immigrants of ancient *Qiang* nationality. Though this merits in-depth research, the configuration and inherent essence of the *Tu Zhang* Dwelling are consistent with the cave abode created by ancient *Qiang* nationality according to spiritual strain. For example, *Hani's Congpopo* (In Hani language, *Congpopo* means moving from one place to another.), an important work of Hani's traditional literature, says directly that six thousand Hani people left hometown, and went toward southern mountains. Now, pan-manitou, ancestor and hero worship left in Yi and Hani nationalities are similar to that of the ancient *Qiang* ancestors of the upper reach of Yellow River. Even central ground, deity forest and village gate in villages have intensive signification. So, people can subtly feel that the *Tu Zhang* Dwelling and the *Tu Zhang* Dwelling village reflect obscure cognition about universe descended from ancestors, and also imply their souls' reposition for ancestors.

There is a legend in Hani's myth: during remote antiquity time, Hani people resided in cave, mountains were high and roads were steep, and it was very inconvenient to work out of house. Afterward, when they came to a place, called *Reluo* , they found big mushrooms all over the mountains and plains, which could withstand wind's blow and rain's

The mushroom houses and the lane in the village.

hit and under which ants nested. Therewith, people constructed mushroom houses. This kind of pan-manitou also incarnates in village's layout. For example, Village Deity Forest which is the abode of the village deity and set up on upper village, should be determined when

There are a lot of ponds in the village and the ponds are surrounded by green trees.

building a village: taking big tree which was out of the village as a sign, or simply using branches to construct village gate aimed to bar tragedy, wickedness and ghosts out of the village; *Mo Qiu* Square, which lied at village corner, was the place for staging the whole village's fete activity. And, Hani people thought that the well's stream, which originated from mountains, is bestowed by mountain deity. If women

The Village Deity Forest beyond the Hani village.

drink it, she would become beautiful. If men drink it, he would become handsome. From these facts, we can see that Yi and Hani people look village as their nationality's safe habitat and shelter, and their spiritual dependence, so they always have very good imagination about the origin of house and village, and in these imagination repose their yearn for good life.

In the *Tu Zhang* Dwelling villages, each family has a fire pit, which was the center for family activities and spiritual reposition as well. The fire pit was set up inside of room, and never extinct, and had a tripod on it, which could hold up pan to fry dish. Commonly, all families drank tea and had dinner around the fire pit, and warmed themselves in winter. Some families set a

The grassy roof, road and green plants form a entirety.

bed for the aged near the fire pit, which represented an ancient relic, called "sleeping around fire". When guests came, hot-hearted host would let them sit around the fire pit, let them take water cigarette for a long time, drink a cup of "sticky rice savory tea", and drink a cup of goluptious "stuffy pan wine". With the alcohol interest, the host would open his voice, singing songs to wish guest lucky. So, the fire pit was tender and affectionate.

The *Tu Zhang* Dwelling and its village have another characteristic – a *Tu Zhang* Dwelling's space is not very big indicating a kind of equilibrium and equality. There is no tall wall and big courtyard, and no alleyway and deep residence, which made people feel comfortable and peaceful. This characteristic shows conspicuous differences with other nationalities' house size and hierarchy distinction, which, however, was determined by Yi and Hani people's family and social structure. As to Hani people, they have still kept paternalistic family structure, in which male played the main role. This paternalistic family seldom had several generations together. Except that the youngest son will live with his parents until they die, other sons should leave well after marriage. So, every generation could divide into several little families, and construct social basic cell. Because of the vertical strain structure for generations, the whole village forms very complex but very clear consanguine relation net and village social structure. This village social structure made people of a clan very united. This kind of concord and harmonious atmosphere in the *Tu Zhang* Dwelling was common. Hani people's "long street banquet" thoroughly represented good feeling among neighbors.

In the morning of New Year, every Hani village would begin the long booze in the center of the village and celebrated the festival symbolizing their comity, concord, luckiness and happiness. People carried square tables to street center to connect one by one, more than one hundred tables were connected to form a 100 meters long dragon. Then, each family used dapper bamboo basket to carry their skillful dishes. At the first glance, there were every specialty from soup to nuts. In this vivid vision, one could not help sighing with feeling the complete harmony among constructions, street and people's life in *Tu Zhang* Dwelling villages.

All the windows of *Tu Zhang* Dwelling were very small, and most of windows using little stout batten as window lattice. When the sky was clear, sunlight shot into across window lattice continuously. The goods in the sunlight were bright and vivid; those goods in shadow flash a layer of dark light, which was antique and mysterious.

The Conversion to Nature

Relationship between *Tu Zhang* Dwelling villages and their natural environment is very harmonious, and *Tu Zhang* Dwelling villages are ecological homesteads fitting for inhabitation. Houses were built along sunny hill slopes, distributed along hillside and layer upon layer. Fountains from mountains flow into village across every house. Green foliages, for example, golden bamboo and brown loquat, were extensively planted, and the environment was clear and mellow. According

The terraces in the morning sunlight.

to a Hani's ancient song, three tiers of palm trees should be planted at village's head, three tiers of golden bamboos should be planted at village's house. Around village, the forest was luxuriant and strongly fragrant. Terraced fields before village extended to hillfoot, and when it is season for transplanting seedlings, water field seems like bright mirrors with brilliant and silver light glittering under the sun.

Terraced fields are masterpiece of Hani people. Since thousands of years, in abnormally hard environment of high mountains and valleys, Hani people had accumulated and created a suit of planting experience and pattern on terraced fields. They built banks according to natural ecological situation, while

having introduced never-dried springs into terraces. In early spring, terraced fields were like clusters of bright pearls spread from the sky; in March or April, layers of terraced fields were like blocks of green

Terrace in the depths of the Ailao Mountains cultivated by the Hani people.

tapestries; in end summer or early autumn, mature paddies were golden yellow. In the Ailao mountain ranges these terraced fields sometimes reach hundreds of stages and stretch around several mountains and the scenery is spectacular. Some scholars said that "the succeess of digging up terraced fields made Hani nationality's social and historical development process changed dramatically, they eventually settled down from rambling-travel furrowing and long time slash-and-burn farming, and produced new living mode and value and philosophy, whose core is terraced-rice-farming culture".

Terraces had melted into Hani peoples' life and they had deep relationship with terraces. There is a folk saying of Ailao Hani nationality, saying that "terrace is chap's face". Whether a chap is handsome is not determined by his appearance but by his tilling skills. If he is well versed in bank's building, mound's shoveling, and land's plough, he should be appreciated by everybody, and would naturally win girl's love. Whether a girl is beautiful or not, is not decided by her appearance, and also partly by whether she can work in terrace.

In fact, Hani people' hardworking and wisdom are not merely exhibited in digging up terraces, and what is more important is that they created terrace culture. The spiritual essence implied by this culture is appreciating nature, conforming to nature and kindly treating nature.

The *Tu Zhang* Dwelling at mountainsides also

The upmost part of the mountain is suitable for grazing, the middle part is suitable to construct dwellings and the fields at the foot of the mountain is ideal for cultivation.

harmoniously melted into the nature eco-system, and found its fit position. That "areas at up mountain are suitable for herding, those at middle mountain are suitable for dwelling and those at down mountains are suitable for furrowing" is the best annotation for this village gathering mode. This village layout was repeatedly mentioned by Hani ancient songs and adages, for example, "Fields should be farmed at mountain foot, babies should be produced at mountainside". "Huge mountain ridge, green mountain, beautiful water, few disaster; dense forest is hard to carve out a way, monsters also do not dare to enter village, all descendants of Hani people love to build village on mountains".

On all Hani villages' backward mountains, there is a tract of green woods, Hani people look it as deity forest, and people pray to it for the peace of village, health of villagers and good harvest of terraces every year. So, protecting mountain forest become their austere and natural hope and request. Hani people also pay attention to harmonious relationship between village population and resources. Their village generally is not very big, has about several hundreds of families. With the population increasing, part of them should be separated from the village, build village basing on the same mode at another mountain, and dig up terraces. This village development mode also indicates local people's comprehension and adaption to the nature on the other hand.

Tu Zhang Dwellings and those sceneries resembles fairyland, villages like a big garden. Like the Ailao mountain people's soul, the *Tu Zhang* Dwelling had melted into the nature and been converted to natural fairyland.

by Wang Dong

8 Comfortable and Harmonious Dwelling Prizing the Culture and Martial Art
— A View of Minxi Dwelling

Minxi (west part of Fujian Province) is surrounded by mountains and far from the noise of industrial civilization, just like the imaginary paradise or Shangri-la in the human world. The picturesque Wuyi Mountain scenic spot attracts the attention of the citizens of modern cities. It is of greater importance to say that here is the homeland of several score millions of Hakkas. Besides, the specific historical and geographic location has nurtured a unique dwelling which is called "clay building" in the Minxi area, everyone having a look at its appearance will gasp in admiration of its beauty.

Hakkas' Homeland

We must mention Hakkas when talking about the Fujian dwelling. Many Hakkas in Minxi area built their uncalcined clay building abode while the existing uncalcined clay buildings are mainly located at the Hakkas settlements. Hakkas who accounted for 6% of the Han population are a branch of the Han nationality. Hakkas's ancestors lived in the Central Plains of China. After the Western Jin Dynasty (265-316), the Hans having suffered from chaos caused by wars gradually migrated southwardly and a number of them immigrated into the place where Jiangxi, Guangdong and

The clay building surrounded by mountains.

The tamping technology.

Fujian Provinces meet. Having gradually integrated with the natives they finally became the "Hakkas" denoting people distinctive from the "natives". Due to the fact that the plains with good environment had already been occupied by other Hans the Hakkas could only settle down in the hilly areas of South Jiangxi Province, West Fujian Province, and East Guangdong Province. Therefore, we may say "every mountain has Hakkas while every Hakkas lived in a mountain".

What we must point out is that not all Hakkas are living in the clay building which is just one kind of Hakkas dwelling, but not the only residential form of the Hakkas. Xie Zhongguang, a famous Chinese scholar pointed out that the uncalcined clay buildings mainly distribute over some regions in Southwest Fujian Province and Northeast

Guangdong Province. Such a kind of clay building, especially the round buildings can hardly be found in other regions. This phenomenon is originated from the geographic and cultural background of the above-mentioned areas.

111

Historically speaking, the Hakkas migrated from north to south or from west to east. Thus, northwest part of west Fujian inhabited by the Hakkas became the core area with Hakkas culture. The muliti-storied clay buildings, however, are rarely seen in this area. Only when you go southward can you find a great deal of clay buildings in the area where the Hakkas lived together with other ethnic groups. In the Ming and Qing dynasties, this area registered frequent fighting with weapons between ethnic groups caused by the acute ethnic disputes. Under such a grim situation the Hakkas had been forced to change their way of life while having moved into the clay buildings with stronger defense functions. Thus, the conclusion can be drawn that the architectural culture of the clay building is part of the brilliant Hakkas culture but not the total of it.

The distribution map of Hakkas in Western Fujian Province.

A Glimpse of Clay Building

The amazing impression at the first glance of the Minxi clay building is the gigantic architectural volume of a building, which could be rarely seen among vernacular dwellings in other parts of China. The distinctive feature of the clay building is its simple body full of geometrical touch. Its body is usually in round or square shape, and sometimes also in shapes of ellipse, the Eight Diagrams, half-moon, polygon. Moreover, the so-called "Five-Phoenix" building having a roof with staggered eaves can be reckoned as

The magnificent round clay building group.

the exception because of its variations of shapes.

Generally speaking, the clay buildings are two to six-storied dwellings with a military defensive hue. On the walls of the first floor there is no window at all, while on the walls of the second floor installed a little number of small windows. So far as the arrangements of architectural function, kitchen and dining room were generally placed on the first floor; the storage rooms were on the second floor; while the bedrooms were placed on the third or higher floors. The base of wall is 3 m thick; the wall of the first floor is 1.5m thick, the thickness of the wall will reduce upward. Inside of the exterior walls, the space was partitioned into several rooms with planks. The rooms were connected to the corridors. In the central part were ancestral hall, private school or stage. Though the clay building was a very closed system, it was a place of unique attraction: all rooms were opened inwardly through connecting the corridors, which had formed into a "central yard" abound in human kindness. When strolling in a clay building you can find the couplets, calligraphies or paintings. Therefore it is worthy of the description that the clay building is gentle inside and looks ruthless from outside.

The Minxi clay buildings are in various shapes and postures. But those of great numbers or wide spread are square, round and five-phoenix buildings.

The "square building" widely distributed over Yongding county is a simple structure while its plane surface is in forms of square, rectangle or the Chinese character "目" shape. The most popular square building is the *Yijing* dwelling in Guopo Town, Yongding County. Built in the first year of the reign of Xianfeng, the Qing Dynasty (1851) the *Yijing* dwelling had a construction area totaling 4000 m², which was completed within more than 70 years by people of three generations and was called "*Da Lou Sha*" locally. The exterior wall is 136 m long in eastern and western directions, while 76 m in the southern and northern directions with a portal and two side entrances. The whole building is composed of four parts: a five-

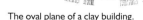

The oval plane of a clay building.

The protruding attic of the clay building which is for the purpose of shooting conveniently.

storied building in the back, three four-storied buildings in the left, right and front respectively. The four parts form the shape of the Chinese character " 口 " while there were buildings also in the shape of the Chinese character "口" inside. Then the general arrangement of the buildings was in a form of Chinese character " 回 ". The center of the building was a central hall while the left and right wings of the front building were class rooms of a school.

The "round building" is the most famous Minxi clay building, it made the clay buildings hidden in the mountains for several centuries famous to the outside

The magnificent rectangle clay building.

The front gate of *Yijing* Building.

world. The shapes of the round building can be divided into the flat arrangement of monocycle, multi-ring and even the circular linked with square. Multi-ring-structured building could be easily found, while their plane is the concentric circle. The exterior structure is usually high while its internal structure is low. The hall locates in the center of the whole building. It was the public place for weddings, funerals and other celebrations. According to the incomplete statistics, there are more than 360 round buildings in the Yongding County, among them including the oldest "*Chengqi* Building" with the most numerous circles;

the "*Shenyuan* Building" with the longest diameter and "*Rusheng* Building" with the shortest diameter, etc.

Located at the Gaotou Township, Yongding County,

The inner courtyard of *Yijing* Building.

Chengqi Building's scale is astonishing with its diameter about 73m long and circumference nearly 229.34 m. The whole building has 400 rooms where more than 400 people of 60 households live. In 1981 this building was listed in *the Dictionary of China's Scenic Spots* and was known as "king of clay building". The plane arrangement of the "*Chengqi* Building" is "a center with three circular structures": the external circular structure has four storeys, 72 rooms each; the second circular structure has two storeys, 40 rooms each; while the third circular structure only has one storey with 32 rooms; in the middle of the building is the ancestral hall.

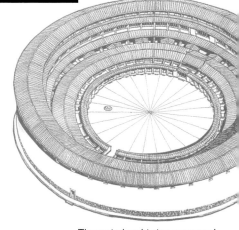

The typical multi-ring-structured round clay building.

116

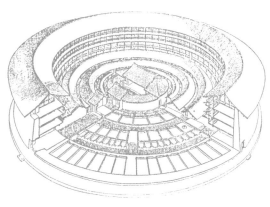

The typical multi-ring-structured round clay building.

The "*Wufeng* (five phoenixes) Building" is a special kind of clay building. Among the clay buildings, *Wufeng* Building is a kind of building most similar to the courtyard dwelling of Northern and Central China. Mainly situated at the core area of Hakkas culture, the *Wufeng* building is a derivative of the quadrangle folk house of the central plains in the special circumstance of Fujian Province and has reflected the influence of the feudal ethical code of the central plains.

The *Chengqi* Building having withessed numerous historical changes.

The splendid *Wufeng* Building.

The typical structure of *Wufeng* Building is characterized by three halls accompanied with two horizontal buildings with distinct axis, and the front part being low and the back part being high, while facing the Sun and with its back to the river. The three halls are the lower hall, the central hall and the main building, the two horizontal buildings are the rectangular architectures located at both sides of three halls. Such a courtyard arrangement is similar to that of the central plains. The mountain slope being high in the north and low in the south was chosen as the building site. Thus the whole architectural group

117

The roof of the *Wufeng* Building is like a phoenix spreading its wings.

ascends from the south to the north. Viewing from the front the roofs present many levels full of grandeur. In the areas where the *Wufeng* dwellings were built the feudal ethics were widely spread among the people, who longed to get scholarly honor and official rank through reading books or obtain glory for the whole community. The *Wufeng* Building sometimes is called "*Dafuti*-styled clay building" because a horizontal

The *Fuyu* Building.

board inscribed with three Chinese characters Da Fu Di was hanged on the gate of the building. Aside from the role of parading the distinguished status, this kind of Chinese characters was a metaphor for building owner's ambition to long for high position and wealth through imperial examinations.

The *Fuyu* building at Hongkeng Village of Hukeng Town in Yongding County is a typical *Wufeng* Dwelling. The construction began in 1880 by three brothers of Lin clan, this building occupied an area of 7000 M². The central axis of the *Fuyu* Dwelling is low in front and high in back; two horizontal buildings were arranged on both wings of the principal building; in front of the building there are three gates. Judging from its appearance, the principal building and the horizontal houses are well combined. The gate level ground and walls were paved or built with cobblestones. The buildings were ingeniously constructed and integrated with the surroundings. The exterior shape of the building is just like three mountains, which means that the three brothers who owned the building were like the three magnificent mountains.

As for the clay buildings of other shapes, the plane arrangements are also colorful, for instance, the ellipse shape, the half-moon shape and the polygon shape, etc. The *bagua (The Eight Diagrams – eight groups of whole or broken lines used in divination.)* building is worth mention. It is not a simple eight diagrams, but contains the in-depth cultural symbol of the Chinese tradition. In the western part of Fujian Province, site selection and location of the clay building could not be separated from the Eight Diagrams; while some clay buildings copied the images of the Eight Diagrams. This is the origin of the *bagua* dwelling. Some planes of the *bagua* building took the shape of the standardized octagons, for instance, the "*Daoying* Building". But there were circular-shaped *bagua* building while only its arrangement reflected the ideas of the Eight Diagrams. The "*Zhencheng* Building" at the Hongkeng Village of Hukeng Town in Yongding County is the typical mode of this kind of clay building.

Newly established in 1912 by the brothers of the Lin clan, *Zhencheng* Building occupied an area of 5000 m² while its flat surface can be divided into the internal circle and external circle. The outer ring building is a four-storied structure of the Eight Diagrams (eight combinations with 6 rooms each, on each floor totaling 48 rooms) in circular shape: Each *gua* (combination) of six rooms is an independent unit with a staircase. The *gua*s are separated by the fire-sealing gables and connect by arch doors, which would be closed if one *gua* caught fire. Then, the whole building could escape the fire. The inner ring building is a bi-level structure in which Western architectural styles were applied. The introduction of Western culture could not be separated from the owners of the buildings, the Lin clan enriched themselves in Western countries and were deeply influenced by the Western culture. The building is composed of one hall, two wells (symbolizing the Yin and Yang poles in the Eight Diagrams), three gates (symbolizing the Heaven, Earth and human beings in the Eight Diagrams) and 8 units (Eight Diagrams). Viewing from the above-mentioned we can find that the builders adopted an original approach. Because Chinese and Western styles combined and they supplemented and enriched each other, the building mode of *Zhencheng* Dwelling was sent to the World Architectural Fair, Los Angles of the United States, and was acclaimed as "oriental architectural pearl".

The inner hall of *Zhencheng* Building, a perfect combination of Chinese and Western architectural styles.

Tracing Back to the Source

After a glimpse at the charming colorful posture we cannot but thinking: what's the origin of these clay buildings? How could they evolve into present images? This is a very complicated problem that many scholars have divergent views. Their main views are as follows:

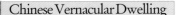

First, the basic feature of the clay building is the "living together" of the whole clan, which is similar to the traditional living way of the Hans in the central plains of China. The clay building was well equipped while beaming a clan atmosphere like a small society. The head of the clan was chosen from the elders who should be of noble character and high prestige. The flat surface of the clay building is characterized by symmetry with explicit building centre while having reflected strong hierarchal ideas. Such a kind of arrangement embodied the patriarchal clan ideology while being in line with the management and control of the conglomerated clan. In terms of technology, though a great deal of ramming technologies were applied, the construction of the clay building was not divorced from the timber-framed building system popular in the Central Plains, while it could be called a branch of architectural culture of the Chinese dwellings.

The wood structure system of the clay building.

In spite of the fact that the ancestors of the Hakkas were the Hans in the Central Plains it was inevitable in the long process of their migration that their culture including language, costume, living habits exchanged with the natives in the southern part of China. The cultural variation emerged in comparison with the orthodox culture of the Central Plains. Moreover, Many Hakkas settlements formed the autonomous management model like the minority nationalities – a trend of native-orientation. Although the Hakkas claimed themselves as the

The mountain village relics distributed in Zhangzhou.

The *Jinjiang* Building in Zhangzhou region which looks like a blockhouse.

descendants of the Hans, the central authorities always treated them as a minority nationality, who were always called "southern barbarian". In the course of suffering from political oppression, military suppress and cultural bias, the Hakkas armed themselves with strong consciousness of self-defense. Besides, the mix of local ethnic groups led to uninterrupted conflicts and because of limited governmental management many Hakkas could not but live in the fortified clay dwellings for safety's sake.

As for the emergence of the round clay building, Huang Hanmin who has studied the clay buildings for many years, pointed out that the round clay building could be traced back to the dwelling of Zhangzhou region of Fujian Province, near the Minxi Hakkas-inhabited region. The Hakkas had learned building technologies from them. Therefore the round buildings were widely distributed over the west part and the south part of Fujian Province. Historically the Zhangzhou area was affected by chaos resulting from civil wars. Then the round castles or mountain villages situated on the mountain tops emerged here and there and finally evolved into the round clay dwellings. At the initial stage the Hakkas lived in the *Wufeng* Buildings, which were similar to the residential in the central plains. In the process of eastward migration, in other words, after they settled down at the juncture of three provinces, Fujian, Jiangxi and Guangdong and for the sakes of survival and security they had learned the constructing methods of the clay building of Zhangzhou area, their shapes of residence gradually simplified while its function of self-defense was strengthened, in other words, they had undergone the process from *Wufeng* dwelling to square building and finally to round building.

Moreover, some scholars are inclined to explain the origin of the round building in terms of cultural orientation. In their opinion, in order to seek lucky, safety and wealth the designer of the round building mixed the Eight Diagrams and diagram of the universe into the designs of the buildings, which finally evolved into the round plane.

Intergrowth with the Human Affection and Reason

Aside from prizing culture and encouraging martial spirits, the Minxi clay building is characterized by *Qingli* (human affection and reason) which embodied the relations of organic integration and close intergrowth between human beings and the environment. In this text *Qing* means perception while it pays more attention to the humanism, which extended as "mood concept in meaning". *Li* means reason, emphasizing on material and technique, which may extend as ecological concept. In Chinese traditional farming community, good mood was embodied in the warm and tender human relationships of the clan settlement; in the traditional clan consanguinity and neighborhood relationship which pay attention to education and culture; in the aesthetic viewpoint inclining to the destination of one's life and harmony; and in the prizing of the moral conduct of feudalism. The good ecological concept was embodied in the structure of building reflecting the ecological balance and paying attention to earth and forest protection, etc.

The whole family live together, which is full of pleasure.

With respect to the mood, the people living in the clay building were honest beings while they were closely associated with solidarity and friendship and maintained the traditional clan group settlement. At the first sight, the arrangement of the clay building was similar to the modern dormitory, but the buildings were beaming with close consanguinity and fratenal affection with which the modern dormitory can hardly compare.

With respect to paying attention to education and culture, the Hakkas have inherited a good historical tradition, for instance, the numerous ancestral halls, studies, horizontal inscribed-boards and calligraphies in the clay building are

The agreeable micro climate environment inside the clay building.

soundlessly telling us their fact. The *Zhencheng* Building with high cultural value could be a good example. Having adopted the ideas of the Eight Diagrams and European architectural styles, the building had well combined the Chinese tradition with Western styles, while inside the buildings were full of strong cultural atmosphere. For example, it was easy to find couplets hung on the pillars of a hall and inscriptions inside the *Zhencheng* building.

In terms of ecological protection, being typical of the clay building, the Minxi clay building reflected the ecological ideas that when human beings developed through full utilization of natural resources, they should reduce the damage to the nature. The clay buildings were built with clay but not bricks, thus the arable land could be well protected; in other words, the building materials of a clay building were drawn from the land, they would regress into the land. In the

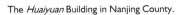

The *Huaiyuan* Building in Nanjing County.

meantime, the thick clay walls had certain advantages such as high capacity for heat accumulation. Therefore the temperature in the clay building was delightful in all seasons. The ring-shaped building arrangement formulated a big yard that was beneficial to wind-rising while the reasonable combination of doors, windows and corridors formulated a good climate environment. As a saying goes that "the clay building can not be burnt by fires and destroyed by the gunfire; it is difficult for bandits to enter and will not fall during the earth-quake". In the perspectives of modern civilization the clay building really has scientific reasoning and contains the simple ecological conception.

If the harmonious mode resulted from the clan harmony or family harmony; and if the external adaptability resulted from good interaction between human beings and external environment, then, does the clay building's intergrowth of affection and reason not only let people feel fresh and new but also add some new enlightenment?

by Yu Feng

9 Magnificent and Beautiful Dwellings
— A Description of Tibetan Watchtower

Tibet is situated at the snow-covered plateau with very clear azure sky and snow-covered peaks rising higher one after another. Here, Tibet is distinct not only for its vigorous and mystical landscape but also for its magical Tibetan culture attracting the people. The geographic traits of the Tibet Plateau have given rise to peculiar human landscape and natural environment.

Tibet is called "roof of world", because it is a plateau with the highest altitude in the world. Tibet owns a wide variety of localized climates and distinct vertical climate zones including high plateau frigid zone, sub-high plateau frigid temperate zone, hilly temperate zone, mountain sub-tropical and mountain tropical zones.

The national culture and diversified geographical environment and distinct climate in the snow-covered plateau of Tibet had given rise to majestic and glorious forms of the Tibetan vernacular dwellings.

A History of Distant Source and Long Stream
About 10,000 years ago there were human footprints on the Tibetan Plateau. According to the archaeological survey all kinds of stone artifacts, bone implements and pottery ranging from the Old Stone Age to the New Stone Age were excavated,

The landform of the Lhasa River valley.

which has proven that the Tibetan people had entered the New Stone Age about 4,000 years ago. The Tibetan vernacular dwellings also saw a history of distant source and long stream. As early as 4,000-5,000 years ago, cave dwellings or semi-cave dwellings or primitive village appeared in Tibet. The excavation of the ruins of Karuo primitive village in Changdu in 1975 has revealed the living conditions of the Tibetan ancestors.

Nationalities including Tibetans, Monbas, Lhobas, Hans and Huis have lived on Tibet Plateau generation after generation among which Tibetans accounted for 94.7%. The Monba nationality is one of the minority nationalities living on Tibet Plateau since the ancient

The landform of the Niyang River valley.

Looking up at Mt Qomolangma from *Rongbu* Temple.

times. Her name was derived from their living place of Menyu Area. The elevation of the Menyu Area is decreased from 4,000 odd meters to 1,000 odd meters. In the 17th century, some of the Monba living in the Menyu area immigrated eastward to Baimagang (now Medog County). From then on the inhabited region of the Monba nationality was composed of the eastern and western areas where two different styles of Tibetan vernacular dwellings were engendered.

The Lhoba nationality composed of more than 30 tribes are mainly living in the south of the big turn of Yarlung Zangbo River. This area is called

Luoyu geographically. In the myths of the Lhoba people, their ancestors ever lived on trees or in the cave dwellings. Before the democratic reform in 1959 the Lhobas still lived in a patriarchal stage of the primitive society. They lived together in line with blood lineages of their tribe or family, which also caused a great impact on the distinct vernacular dwellings.

The distinct cultures of Tibetans, Monbas and Lhobas fall into the same cultural category because they believed that they were all descendants of the divine monkey and the rock demon in accordance with the mystic tales. The three cultures are the integral parts of the culture of the snow land. Similar cultural backgrounds and mutual communications among them had cultivated the same orientation of their dwellings tallying with the local condition such as climate and topographies and in line with their religious beliefs and cultural habits.

Graceful and Colorful Forms of Tibetan Vernacular Dwellings

The watchtower, yak tent, earth house, wood house, bamboo house and plateau cave, and so on have enriched the shape of colorful folk houses because of the vast territory of Tibet Plateau varied in geographical environment, climate features and resources status. In terms of dwelling's structure, they can be divided into styles like earth building, stonework, composite structure of earth, stone and wood,

The scene of dancing.

ganlan and *Jinggan*. Viewing from the forms of the dwellings, they can be classified as flat-roof folk house, sloping roof house and composite-roof house. The diversified Tibetan vernacular dwellings distributed in different regions of Tibet have their regional characteristics. For instance, the nomads of Northern Tibet mainly live in yak hair tents made from long coarse hair of the yak that is woven into strips by nomad women on back-strap looms. Generally speaking, the surface of the tent is in square or rectangle shape with a wood-supporting frame in a height of about two meters with sloping roof covered with black yak hair carpets while four directions are fixed on land with yak hair ropes. A crack about 15cm wide and 1.5m long on the main ridge of the tent is specially designed for day-lighting, ventilating and letting out smoking. Along the crack hanging a number of small hooks which can be used to open or close the crack depending on the weather. The highland barley, butter bags and cow dung could be placed on a wall 40-50 cm in height built with straw earth bricks or adobes inside the tent. One direction of the tent has a door for people's passing in and out; during the daytime, the door curtain will be opened; while the door curtain will be fastened at night so that people inside the tent can enjoy their leisure life. Near the door curtain inside the tent stands the stone fire pit and behind of the fire pit is the place for worshiping Buddha images. Such a yak hair tent made from the coarse hair of the yak is suitable to a nomadic pastoral mode of production. They can be easily taken down and put up when moving camp. They keep out the rain and snows.

The stone-built watchtower-style verracular dwelling.

The watchtower-style dwelling of nobleman.

Another most common dwelling is watchtower, which is built from earth or stone. It is usually called

watchtower because it is shaped like a fort.

The watchtower was usually two or three-storeyed building with stone exterior walls. The watchtowers for noblemen, slave owners and rich merchant were the constructions of more than three storeys, while the highest one even reached to five storeys. The plane of a watchtower was assembled with the column grid as its unit to form square rooms. In the plane, a big room was located at outside while two small rooms were constructed inside, the staggered rooms form an overlapping structure. Its structural system was a composite structure with walls made of timber and stone and columns of timber. One living room had one column, which was locally called "an umbrella" while the floors were paved with planks; the sun-dried mud bricks were 40-80 cm thick while the thickness of the stone walls would extend to 50-80 cm. The interior walls were kept in vertical posture while the exterior would be inclined to entasis. The ground floor of the watchtower was mainly used for animal breeding or for storage. The second or third floor was for people to live, while the balcony or sanitary room made from woods on the second floor was cantilevered. The sunny exposure of a building always had a big window or down-to-floor glass windows, which had advantages of good daylighting. Moreover, windows had advantages of keeping the wind or cold in check, and making the rooms warm in winter and cool in summer because they were opened to the courtyard. Flat roof made of compacted weathered earth

The watchtower-style dwelling with one yard.

The single-floor vernacular dwelling with one yard.

was commonly used for the roofing of a watchtower, while personal effects could bask on the roof balcony.

In the courtyard of the one-coutyard watchtower usually laid a well and planted with flowers. The thick walls of buildings or courtyard were mainly for defense. There is usually a small yard for daylighting. A large-scale watchtower has many rooms, a high watchtower in 20-30 meters was for keeping valuables or for looking into the distance in defense battle. The shapes of the watchtowers varied in different regions. The vernacular dwellings of Lhasa were two or three-storeyed tetrastoa. Of course there were also independent bungalows . The opening bed room with side corridor was the common structure of vernacular dwellings in Shan'nan Prefecture because the people there prefer outdoor exercises.

Many ethnic nationalities are living in the forest area of the southeast Tibet where there are numerous types of folk house. This area is abundant in environment resources while almost all main plant species from tropical to the frigid zones of northern hemisphere can be found here. People like to live in the folk house with a double-slope roof. In the forest area people prefer to live in the detached dwellings or one-courtyard houses. Most of the architectures are three-storied buildings. The first floor was used for animal breeding, the second floor was the dwelling space composed of living room(also served as kitchen), storage room, side corridor and toilets. The living room was separated into two parts by planks. In the middle part of the outer living room stood the fire pit (near the window) surrounded by beds and other furniture. The pediment space under the sloping roof on the third floor was used for storage of straw, fodder, odds and ends like a garret. The buildings were constructed with wood frame. The construction materials included crushed stone, rag-stone, cobblestone, rammed earth, plank, bamboo fence and wicker fence, etc. The pitched roof uses wood girders and rafters placed on the gable, while in the forest area the roofing was usually covered with wood tiles with heavy stones on them to prevent the wood tiles from being lifted by the strong wind. In the area of shale mountain, the roofs were covered with shale tiles against rains.

In the dense forest area of the southeast Tibet the wood houses of Monbas and wood and bamboo houses of Lhobas set each other off. The wood houses of Monbas were built upon the tableland facing the valley. The house is off the ground and supported by many columns with 1.5-2 meters open space for animal breeding in the lower part. The upper part of the house was mainly designed for people's living

132

The vernacular dwelling in Gongbu of Southeast Tibet.

The wood vernacular dwelling in Southeast Tibet.

and storage. The living room in the middle on the second floor has a small passage hall connected to the outer corridor. The two wings of the living room were storage houses. Almost all the building material from walling and flooring to roofing were woods, people can go upstairs or downstairs through the wood stairs. The detached dwellings of the Monbas usually have no walls surrounding them. The stone houses of Cuona County and the wood houses of Medog County belong to the folk house having no courtyard walls and form villages.

The Lhobas have two kinds of distinct traditional dwellings. One is called long house, while the other is a small square dwelling. The long house, a unique dwelling is the embodiment of the primeval social form of the Lhoba tribe. The length of long house often reached several scores of meters. The long house for female to live in was always built on the outside of a village. Planks and bamboo mats were used to separate the long house into ten or several scores of living rooms. The long house for male to live in was often constructed in the middle of a village. Its interior space was not separated, which was a place for discussing the public affairs. The small square dwelling was the couple's dwelling which was a symbol of Lhoba family and was surrounded by warehouses. The raw timber often served as the building materials of the long house or small square dwelling. The wall of the living room was made of logs. There are wood columns for supporting at the lower part of the house while its upper part is covered with plantain leaves roof.

The bamboo house of the Lhobas is in the shape of rectangle, about 6 m wide and 9 m long. A door was located at its entrance while windows were built on the opposite wall for ventilation. The bamboo house was built upon the stone foundation with a wood column every two meters, while double-skin bamboo clappers were used between columns as the wall body. The roof was also covered with bamboo clappers. Except for the floor, girders and column, the whole house was made of bamboos. In front or back of the bamboo house was always attached with standing grain storage.

In the valley plains of Nagri Prefecture of western Tibet the folk house is mainly a detached construction with wood frames. The majority of the vernacular dwellings are two-storied buildings. The first floor is the living place in winter while the second floor is for people to live in summer. The vernacular dwellings adjacent to the foot of a rocky mountain are mainly the combination of caves and houses. The house in front and the cave in the back form an integral residential. The plane of the caves in Nagri Prefecture is in square, circle or rectangle shapes. Among them, square cave 2m to 2.2m high is more popular. The cave dwelling is a rare living abode in the Tibet Plateau.

The villas or estate of noblemen are special kind of plateau dwellings. A villa was usually composed of principal building and front courtyard. The plane was in shape of Chinese character "回"with a yard in the middle. The front courtyard was a two-storied building, while to the north of the front courtyard stood the three-storied principal building. The rooms of the principal building are bright with French window in the south. In the villa there were living rooms and reception room of the noblemen, family hall for worshipping Buddha, and a lot of functional rooms for hired laborers or storage. Along with the emergence of estate economy appeared a number of famous estate buildings. The principal building of an estate is as high as five stories while it is luxurious with garden surrounding it and has complete defense system including walls, ditches, and so on, it also had the

The summer villa of Dalai Lama in Norbulingka.

134

prison for punishing serfs.

The colorful types of the dwelling in the land of snow are not fixed model of dwellings of certain area or certain nationality. With the communication and mutual influences between the regions and nationalities every kind of vernacular dwelling had something mingled with each other and has made some variations, which gave rise to a mixture of different styles of building. The splendid culture in the land of snow has been enriching the culture of neighboring regions. And the colorful forms of the dwelling in Tibet had a tremendous influence on the architectural style of the Tibetan folk dwellings in other areas of China.

The divine mountain: Mt. Namjagbarwa.

The vernacular dwelling of Tibetan people in Yunnan Province.

A Land of Bon and Buddhism

Religions once spread throughout the land of snow where all nationalities were religious believers. Some followed the Bon, the native religion of the Plateau while others were the believers of Tibetan Buddhism.

According to Bon religion all things on earth are sentiment beings. The universe, totem, ghosts and gods and witchcraft were worshiped by the Tibetan ancestors while the mountains, rivers, forest, birds and beasts as well as the natural phenomena were venerated by the people of the land of snow. The origins of stone piles, "Siba" sacrificial song and mask of Tibetan Opera can be traced to religious ceremonies or sacrifices-offering of the Bon religion. The legends of holy mountain, sacred water and sacred stone came from the Bon teachings.

The standing stone and *hada*.

Since the middle of the 7th century when Buddhism was introduced into the Tibet Plateau through the central plains and India, it encountered fierce opposition from the Bon lasted for three hundred years. In the course of conflicts, Buddhism had absorbed the gods and ceremonial rites of the Bon while the latter borrowed the teaching from Buddhism. Upon this base, Tibetan Buddhism – a combination of Buddhism and Bon was born. In contrast to the Buddhism prevailed in other regions of China, Tibetan Buddhism was characterized by regional and nationality traits. The sediment of Bon religion on Tibetan psychology and customs gave the contents of natural worship to the Tibetan Buddhism.

The deep religious belief can find expression in the construction of the vernacular dwelling, as well as their communal activities. For instance, a small pagoda often stood at the entrance or at center of a village while the symbols of Buddhist meaning were decorated on the exterior of the vernacular dwelling. The existence of religious culture can easily be found in village dwelling, selection of construction sites, external appearance of dwelling and interior environment in the land of snow. In these areas, vernacular dwellings were the places where human being and gods live together.

The Buddhist images surrounded by incense burner , ritual implement and Tangka painting scroll with Buddhist tales and teachings stand on the important position facing the sun in the principal room of the vernacular building. On the column caps, beams, walls and top of the kitchen range as well as sleeping cushions, small square tables, Tibetan cabinets etc. were decorated with painting of religious themes. All utensils for daily life such as sitting cushions, cups and drinking vessels were painted with religious motifs including the eight precious pattern designs: treasured umbrella, goldfish, flower vase, lotus flower, right white spiral snail, auspicious knot, victorious flag, golden wheel and the auspicious character "卍". In Buddhism, the motifs of Mandala symbolizing universal order and universal geometric projection were carved on boards, flagstones and metal plates hanging on the walls of the dwelling.

The exterior ornaments of the building like yak horn, religious drawing and mirrors, symbolizing the Totem or praying to God for good luck were hanging on the entrance gate of

The vernacular dwelling and the prayer flag.

Tangka Painting.

Goldfish, one of "the eight precious patterns".

building or courtyard. Some accessories of the building reflected that Tibet people were devout Buddhists. In their eyes the rustle of the long narrow flag in wind was like reciting scripture, which could bless the safety of the family. Therefore it is easy to find the flags on the four corners and the upper ridge of the dwelling, while bluestone relief sculpture of Buddha image and the white stone inscribed with six sounds of the sacred Buddhist prayer were placed on window sill, four corners of the house or walls of the courtyard. In the religious beliefs of the Tibetans, color might serve as a religious emblem. For instance, red represents gods with a hot temper, white represents gods with a lenient

character while yellow and gold symbolize the Buddhism and the Kingdom of Heaven. The color selection and application of the walling, cotton curtain and structural parts of the vernacular dwelling were permeated with the significance of worshipping and religious beliefs.

The prayer flags at the entrance of the village.

In a compact community, the entrance and center of the village were the important places where high white prayer flags were set up and pagodas were built. Thus the places for daily religious activities were formed. Wheel-praying is a basic way of self-cultivation of Tibetan Buddhism, while turning the prayer wheel from left to right clockwise is a Buddhist practice. Chains of rotary wheel for people to turn were arranged around a pagoda. It was very interesting to fix the prayer wheels in the village. Inside of open small houses erected at river mouth or inside a village nearly always installed the prayer wheels propelled by the flowing stream water, while prayer wheels moving day and night was blessing the peace and security of both people and village.

The worship for natural spirits like mountains or rivers can easily find expression in the sense of the site-selection and the construction of the folk houses. For instance, according to Lhoba's tradition of construction site selection, three grains of

The village dwellings which are cosy and in harmony with nature.

unhusked rice representing three kinds of domestic animals such as yak, pig and chicken were mixed with more unhusked rice corresponding to the number of family member, which formed three pinches of unhusked rice; The three pinches of unhusked rice would be separately placed on three well-chosen sites and covered with branches and slabstones after the sunset. Before the sunrise of the next day people would go to see whether the grains of the unhusked rise dispersed or mixed with ants, which was taken as bad omen. If the grains of unhusked rice were kept in good condition, this meant that an excellent site suitable to dwelling construction had been found. And a series of rites for house construction would begin.

Homeland Harmoniously Developing with Heaven and Earth

Heaven which controls rainy and fine seasons, bitter cold and hot, as well as wind, forest, rain and snow is the life of the vernacular dwelling; earth which comprises mountains and river, rising and falling of vast territory, timbers and stones is the root of folk house, while the foundation of the construction of vernacular dwelling is people who labor, live and multiply on this land.

The styles of the vernacular dwelling of the snow land were closely related to the geographic environment, weather conditions, communal settlement, way of life, available building materials and mastery of construction

The vernacular dwellings in the village are harmonious with the mother earth.

technology, which originated from seeking for comfortable living and a common view of the natural environment. With the common view of the shelter for their survival, standing between the Heaven and the Earth while being mingled with them, the Tibetan dwelling had became the material and spiritual homeland coexisted with natural environment.

The styles of the Tibetan dwelling were closely relevant to the natural environment. In terms of dwelling's shape, the roofing shape reflected varying amount of the rains; the walling thickness reflected the variation of temperature; the openness or closeness of the distribution told people the conditions of sunshine or wind blowing while the stocky and graceful styles reflected the characteristics of geographic environment. Being situated on the land of snow the fire pit inside the principal room was the living center, which reflected that Tibetans were seeking for more comfortable life. The main ways of production on the land of snow were nomadic roving, agricultural tilling and hunting with close relationship to the natural resources, which has a great impact on the structure of the Tibetan dwelling reflecting the harmonious relation between human beings and nature.

The use and obtain of building materials in Tibet were in line with the principle of convenience and least economic cost.

The building materials of the Tibetan dwelling could be easily taken from the natural environment. The Tibetan dwellings were characterized by obtaining raw materials locally. With the corresponding technical processing, the Tibetan dwellings were built from the indigenous building materials while they look like something grown out of the natural environment. In terms of the color modeling the Tibetan dwellings used the color combinations of the natural color of natural materials including yellow of the earth, green of the stone, dark blown of timbers, which reflected the harmonious relationship between the Tibetan dwellings and natural environment.

The Tibetan dwellings built with natural materials and colors are like the products of nature. In terms of measurement, texture and color the

The natural color of vernacular dwelling.

The vernacular dwelling rooted on the earth and near the sky.

environmental individuality of the Tibetan dwelling was full exploited to the extremity.

The majority parts of the land of snow are areas full of rising and falling mountains belonging to dry and semi-dry territory and arid climate of abundant sunshine and big temperature gap between day and night but not abundant in forest resources.

The stone watchtowers with plane roofs and rammed clay buildings were distributed over the above areas. The thick and heat-preservation walls were constructed with earth and stones in multiple ways. The essential tone of the Tibetan dwelling was the natural color of the earth and stone walls and white of wall coat. In the radiant and enchanting sunlight and under the stainless blue sky stood still the stocky stone watchtower and rammed clay building amid the mountains, which had integrated with the natural environment.

The forest region along the Yarlung Zangbo River of southeast Tibet are characterized by deep gorges covered with dense forest and hot and damp climate. Among the green trees and bamboos stood the wood or bamboo houses with pitched roofs. On the slope land against the mountains and facing the sun stood the light and graceful wood houses, whose opening and empty shape could blow away the sultry and damp air with the aid of strong valley wind while the broad roofs of dwelling could protect the wall from erosion by rain. The *ganlan* and log houses in the forest areas could live together with natural environment relying upon the rich natural building material and waterproofed material like leaves of Chinese banana trees. The bamboo sea spreading all over the mountains and valleys in Luoyu area produces more than bamboo. The high-yield bamboo output has provided the Lhobas abundant building materials for the construction of their dwellings. In the forest areas of Southeast Tibet light and graceful wood and bamboo houses rising against sky standing amid the green forest and graceful bamboo sea formed a beautiful dwelling environment.

A Living Picture Full of Grandeur

The mystical and fascinating land of snow attracts the people with its blue skies, lofty snow-covered mountains, vast grassland, whistling rivers and surging lakes... and the sunlight less forest area of the Southeast Tibet is intertwined with gorges and green forest and grass while being decorated with waterfalls and flying clouds.

The character of Tibetan people has been nurtured while people's temperament on the plateau has been molded by the shape, line and color of the natural environment.

The cultural soul of the Tibetan people is originated from their religious beliefs, emotion, ideals and the living customs while the peculiar individuality of the people on the plateau was molded by the human and natural environments. In the hearts of Tibetan people their adoration of magnificent mountains and river, their cherishment of life on paradise, their pursuit for the beautiful

A village settlement in Lang County.

The village beside the terrace.

spirits of Tibetan Buddhism as well as their respect of graceful environment, their looking for fine and tranquil life and their longing for happy life in Buddhist tales, have forged their aesthetic and cultural feelings. Tibet is a graceful land full of grandeur. Located at a natural and human environment of vast and mystical land, the Tibetan dwelling was not only the manifestation of a lofty and magnificent formation freeing from vulgarity, but also an expression of romantic, elegant and clean shape in terms of its modeling.

The village immerged in mountain and forest.

The watchtowers and rammed earth houses dispersed over the cities and towns, mountains villas and villages attracted people with their stocky, simple and vigorous structure and distinctive and unadorned colors beaming with dignified and lofty grandeur.

The wood and bamboo houses nestling among the forest and bamboo seas have presented the graceful and tranquil scene and easy life with their light and elegant modeling and beautiful colors similar to those of the environment. The terraced fields beside the village, the sounds of singing in the village, the fragrance of wine present us a graceful living landscape with beautiful mountains and rivers.

Such a kind of graceful living landscape just like the words in *Song of Vagrants* of the Monba nationality:

> *I finally returned my beloved homeland,*
> *As I hate to part with the wine fragrance;*
> *I shall never part with the Menyu wood houses,*
> *Because I grudge to give up my wine cup!*
> *I shall never be a vagrant in the alien land again!*

by Fan Xiaopeng

Chinese Vernacular Dwelling | Cultural China Series